A

Heart Full of

Precious Memories

To my very dear friend
& sister in Christ!

I am thrilled God brought

us together and am

looking forward to

future sweet

fellowship!

I love you!

Jilene Williams

A

Heart Full of

Precious Memories

A Delightful Glimpse into a

Mid 20th Century Girl's Childhood

1950s and 1960s

Jilene Williams

For more information,
email address: jilene@jilene.com
website: www.jilene.com

eBook edition June 20, 2020

First paperback edition January 2021
Series: A Lifetime of Heartwarming Memories
Volume One

Blessed Memories Press

ISBN-13: 978-1-7346727-0-1 (Paperback)
ISBN-13: 978-1-734627-1-8 (Large Print Paperback)
ASIN: B08BKLB2MQ (ebook)

Disclaimer: Registered brand names referred to in this memoir do not indicate the owner's endorsement of this book. The names are used only to express memories of personal experiences.

Connect with Jilene
for a Sweet Gift

A Heart Full of Precious Memories has a free companion journal in a downloadable PDF! As memories are jogged, readers have enjoyed jotting down what they experience. Get your copy now or come back later on a reread of the book. It is my gift to you!

www.jilene.com

www.jilene.com/reflections-journal

Email: jilene@jilene.com

Dedication

This book is dedicated

To the glory of my Creator and Savior,
who knit me in my mother's womb and ordered all my days.

To my parents,

who brought me through my childhood and gave me a loving start
in life.

To the wonderful man I met forty-six years ago
because I was not wearing my glasses.
He had just told God that he was through with women
and was perfectly content to remain single.
Neither of us had any idea that we would marry within
seven months or the adventures we would share.
Thank you, Steve Williams,
for your loving encouragement, prodding,
and being a delightful sounding board for every word
written within these pages.
These too, are heartwarming experiences.

To our sons and daughter and their spouses
and the nineteen grandchildren
who bring us so much joy.

To my wonderful family, friends, and acquaintances,
who have encouraged me and have invested in my life,

And finally, to you, the reader.

Quotations

"Let your light so shine before men
that they may see your good works
and
glorify your Father which is in heaven."
Matthew 5:16, KJV[A]

Finally, brethren, whatsoever things are true,
whatsoever things are honest,
whatsoever things are just, whatsoever things are pure,
whatsoever things are lovely, whatsoever things are of good report;
If there be any virtue, and if there be any praise,
think on these things.
Philippians 4:8, KJV[B]

"The world is a brighter place when you warm another's heart!"

— Jilene Williams

Introduction

A Heart Full of Precious Memories is a delightful glimpse into the childhood of a mid-twentieth-century girl in love with life. It was written to answer to a question posed by my grand-daughter, "Gamma, what was it like in the "back thens?" When the opportunity arose, satisfaction to the queries unearthed thoughts long forgotten and so began a trek down the path of memory lane. Distance and time afforded little exchange of these stories over the years, so a desire grew to record the journey.

As the pages unfolded, all kinds of feelings welled up. Smiles followed sweet moments, and laughter erupted at times. Tender scenes brought gentle tears, while fearful encounters brought speculation and acute reactions. Victory brought a sense of accomplishment, and failures left unanswered questions. All this and more comes as the tiny tow-headed toddler grabs the readers' heartstrings, until she becomes a preteen sporting tennis shoes. There is much to enjoy along the way.

Table of Contents

Life on the Corner

of

Page and Delaware

1 - Rise and Shine Sleepy Head

In the early morning, a curly blonde-headed toddler lay deeply asleep. She awoke to the sound of her Mommy, calling her into the first daylight, "Rise and shine, Sissie Zene! It is time to get up and see your daddy!"

Her mother gently lifted her from the bed, and after a tight hug, she released her to the floor. Jilene wobbled a bit, trying to find her footing. In seconds, she enthusiastically ran toward the sound of running water in the bathroom with great anticipation crying, "Daddy, Daddy, Daddy!!!" Reaching the open door, she hurried to the lid of the toilet and climbed to her position next to her dad. She leaned onto her podium, which consisted of the edge of the sink. Avoiding the shaving mug full of homemade shaving cream, she got as close to him as she possibly could. She peered into his face, anticipating their heart-to-heart exchange. Her daddy's twinkling eyes remained affixed on his reflection in the mirror as he prepared for the conversation, which was about to begin. With the keenness of a young newspaper reporter, she gleefully interrogated him. Not missing a stroke of his razor, the tall man with thinning blond hair hung on every word.

As if she was in hot-pursuit on the trail of a headlining story, she queried, "Daddy!?! Are you shaving?"

"Yes, Honey, I am shaving."

A few seconds passed. "Daddy? Are you shaving?"

"Yes, Honey, I am shaving."

Again, "Daddy? Are you shaving?"

"Yes, Honey, I am shaving!"

Moments passed. "Daddy? Are you shaving?"

With the great bravado of a seasoned actor, he delivered his well-calculated response. Raising the shaving brush loaded with suds toward his mouth, he declared, "No, Honey! I am eating ice cream!!!"

Jilene bailed off of that toilet lid as fast as she could, screaming as she ran down the hall, "Mommy, Mommy, Mommy!!! Daddy's eating shaving cream!"

The early morning daddy-daughter date was a delightful routine. Our conversations created great enthusiasm and rewards for the lines for future stories.

Two more verbal exchanges made the hall of family fame soon after. According to Dad, I came running into the bathroom in my usual manner, seeking the answer to my question of the day. Dad, in his usual place, was going through his shaving ritual. Positioned at my podium, as eloquently as a three-year-old could muster, I presented him with my query, "Daddy? Are you my daddy?"

Without a pause, he replied, "Yes, Honey, I am your daddy!"

"Daddy? Are you my daddy?

"Yes, Honey, I am your daddy!"

Undoubtedly persistent, I presented my inquiry one last time. "Daddy? Are you my daddy?"

"No! I am your uncle Pete!!!"

That, evidently, rendered me quite speechless as I mulled over his response. The ramifications of a father's words to an incredibly trusting toddler became quite a burden. No way could he convince me that he was my daddy as I quite believed his every word. For months, when we were together in public, it was "Uncle Pete" who escorted me, Mom, and my baby sister! I called him "Uncle Pete" and would not have it any other way. After all, he insisted that he was my uncle Pete, and who was I to question his words?

The matter was finally settled, and I returned to calling, "Uncle Pete," "Daddy." Those precious bathroom conferences continued for quite a while.

The third story he loved to share was about his question to me! He waited until I was in a pensive state of mind and brought me out of it with, "Zene? Are you mean?"

By this time, I had outgrown the need for the repeated exchanges. In shock and disbelief that Daddy would ask me such a cruel question, I defiantly quipped, "No, Daddy, I am precious!"

Dad loved to share these and so many other stories about my sisters and me. When he did, it was with a gleam in his eyes and pride in his heart. I still hear the laughter of his voice in my mind from so very long ago! I wish that I could share just one more conversation with my first love.

2 - Home Sweet Home

Soon after I was born, we moved to Kansas City, Missouri, for a year. In 1954, we returned to St. Louis before my sister, Terri, was born.

Our parents bought a house in Wellston at the corner of Page Boulevard and Delaware Avenue[1]. The house number was 6300. It was built during the suburban expansion west of St. Louis in the early 1900s and was at least 50 years old when they purchased it.

Our house was built above a concrete-walled basement whose height reached three feet above ground. Those walls inset with three small windows were painted white. The two-storied structure had a finished attic. A hip roof with hip roof dormers and a twelve-foot tall chimney completed the home.

The outside walls were covered with asphalt shingles designed to look like varying shades of dark red brick. White wooden shutters flanked the wood-framed windows on the first and second floors. The front of the house had two joined windows to the left of the front entrance. Above them and parallel were another two joined windows and one window directly above the front door. The remaining windows on the sides and back were placed in accordance with the interior use rather than a pleasing outward appearance.

In the back of the house, large porches on the first and second floors were enclosed, and as time passed, converted into finished rooms. A staircase on the back led from the first floor to the backyard surrounded by a white picket fence. Beyond this was the old carriage house.

The front of the house faced north, and three concrete steps from the front sidewalk led to the porch. The mailbox and front door were on the right. A decorative light blue half rail flanked the porch, which was large enough to accommodate four folding chairs. A lawn providing plenty of room to play tag or hurl softballs or snowballs separated the property from the street.

3 - The Front Yard

Until I was five, the porch across the front of the house was a great gathering place for the family to enjoy early evenings after dinner. Friends and neighbors joined us for polite conversation and passing of time. While adults relaxed and watched the activities on the corner, Terri and I played in the front yard.

As the street lights lit, we feasted on the visual delights of the early evening. Lightening bugs floated delicately to and fro across the lawn. Occasionally, they were temporarily held hostage in jars with holes punched in the lids to make lanterns and released before retiring for the evening. Sometimes, bats were spotted flying high above the lights in search of bugs that were attracted there. It was interesting to see them but also a little unnerving.

Soon we were shuttled into the house to get ready for bed and tucked in for the night. Our beds were in the front room near the open windows. It was hard not to want to rejoin the adults if they continued their conversations on the porch. I strained my ears as best I could to snatch a few words here and there, but alas, my heavy eyelids drug me into a deep sleep.

The daylight gave a totally different perspective to our front yard. A cheery pink seven sister rose bush welcomed everyone from the stairs to the porch. The sidewalk leading to the side street gave ample room for jump rope and hopscotch. Along its edge was a row of pink, yellow, orange, violet, white, and red rose moss in the summer. In a row behind them, a variety of tulips in burgundy, pink, red, yellow, and purple were intermingled with pink and purple hyacinths in the spring. Pink, orange, yellow, and red zinnias lined the Delaware Avenue side of the house.

Bushes edged the outside perimeter of the yard, and a short white fence along the front separated the yard from the street parking, the bus stop, and the old olive drab colored United States Post Office box. The most beautiful red maple tree in the world was on the northeast corner of our lot. It almost defied being near the intersection of a four-lane highway and a two-lane through street.

I loved watching that tree go through the cycles of budding tender red and green leaves, and then watching the delicate seeds shaped like tiny propellers falling off only to be caught up by the wind in the spring. Occasionally, cardinals or robins lit in its branches. In the summer, it was dressed with vibrant emerald green leaves, which turned to yellow, orange, red and brown and fell to the ground in autumn. The lofty tree was a resting place for the snow that laid so comfortably on its strong branches in the winter. It seemed to be secretly and silently enjoying all of the activities while emitting a sense of protection, comfort, and happiness.

Along the east side of the yard were a few more bushes and a patch of bachelor buttons in blue and purple hues. During the summer, yellow dandelions and white clover dotted the lawn. Mom called them weeds. However, I loved picking the yellow flowers and watching the tiny dandelion seeds take flight. White clover flowers became chain necklaces, bracelets, and crowns for little princesses to pass summer afternoons. When the grass grew tall enough to go to seed, the fuzzy tails of the stems smelled good and tickled our noses when we played with them. We often picked a stem and chewed on it because it was sweet tasting.

When we were old enough, we harvested all the seeds from the rose moss and picked weeds and eventually learned to mow the lawn with the old wooden sickle push mower in the summer. We learned to rake leaves in the fall and shovel snow in the winter. It was hard to keep our balance on the icy sidewalk. The front yard was a tranquil corner on the otherwise busy boulevard.

Around the House

4 - Life on the First Floor

Our house was converted into five separate living quarters. We lived on the first floor with the entry to our "home" at the end of a long hallway from the front door to a single French door. On the inside, the glass was covered with tightly gathered sheer curtains to block the view.

The first room entered was the kitchen, the liveliest of all the places in the house. It was decidedly multifunctional, maintaining its natural function, and several other activities as needed.

A white built-in corner cabinet to the right displayed Mom's good dishes in the upper section behind a white framed glass door. She had her collection of salt and pepper shakers on the middle shelf. These trinkets recorded her travels across the United States over several years. A twirling porcelain ballerina and a clock under a glass dome took center stage on the top shelf. The clock and a mirror in the living room were gifts from her brother while he was on active duty in the army in Germany during WWII. The lower cabinet housed more utilitarian objects related to Mom's sewing projects.

There was a unique, almost secret joy I felt in the kitchen on tranquil summer afternoons. The window on the west wall was the only outside ventilation, which also became a precious stage entrance for delightful experiences. The elderly couple who lived next door kept a beautiful garden of flowers and vegetables. Huge black walnut trees at the back of their property shaded our house and theirs. Every so often, a gentle breeze danced through the branches, collecting breath-taking scents of the garden. Soft beams of sunlight filtered through the glorious green leaves. Together the air and the light waltzed cheerfully through the window, spilling into the room. I soon found my little fingers chasing sunbeams across the kitchen table's surface with great delight. Those brief encounters felt like loving smiles and tender hugs from God! Moments like those are oases in everyday life.

So on with the furnishings in the rest of the room. A nearly obsolete refrigerator stood five feet tall next to the window. It predated the frost-free models, and its use became the cause for some very stern remarks. Often, Mom or Dad's voice rang out, "Know what you want before you open that door! Get in, get it, get out, and shut that door!" That statement cannot be fully appreciated until one personally defrosts a cumbersome old refrigerator. The frost in the freezer compartment expanded rapidly into thick sheets of ice. Each time the door was opened, warm air rushed in, melting a thin layer. Close the door, and another layer of ice formed. The cycles repeated, crowding out the space for food and aluminum ice cube trays. It was one job that was a constant wrestling match.

A space of about three feet gave access to the southern wall filled with white enameled metal cabinets. A big white porcelain cast iron sink was mounted on the counter. It was molded with a ribbed drainboard on its right side. Besides the everyday kitchen duties, Mom did her home permanents and washed our hair there. She picked us up and plopped us on our backs on the ribs of the drainboard with our heads hanging face up over the edge. Somehow she completely missed out on the gentleness gene. The activity was rarely met without resistance from the victims. The best thing about her washing our hair was when it was over, and we were freed!

Highly motivated to learn how to wash her own hair, my sister would say, "I dood it by myself!"

The remaining counter space was home to an electric percolating coffee pot, and a lard can. Four turquoise enameled canisters with cream-colored lids anchored the corner. Mom stored her coffee, sugar, and "treats" in them. Now, treats to most people, do not include dry macaroni or dry rice. For some crazy reason, I loved to get those last two items and let them soften in my mouth. Mom preferred these staples were left for meals and began hiding them. I often waited until she went to see our neighbor, Dorothy, and climbed up on the counter and searched for my "treats." I took a butter knife, pried the lid off the canister, and absconded the rice grains or macaroni. With determined precision, I restored them to their proper places in the cabinets. I confess that this was wrong. Patience was a virtue I lacked in my childhood.

Rounding the corner was the old gas range. It had two burners and a warming tray on the top. A broiler oven sat under the regular oven on the right, and two storage drawers for pots and pans were on the left. Mom was vigilant to keep us away from the kitchen when she used the broiler. Yet I enjoyed listening to the meat or desserts sizzle under the heat behind the open broiler door.

A rolling pin covered with a crocheted sleeve and two screwed in metal hooks held potholders above the range. A square red electric clock with a cream-colored face and black hands and numbers kept us on time. I liked that old clock a lot. Eventually, Mom replaced it with an orange and black kitty-cat clock. Its tail and eyes moved as the minutes passed.

The kitchenette stationed in the remaining corner of the room was purchased in 1957. Mom was quite impressed with its chrome legs and rim. The top was a speckled black, gray, and white low-maintenance formica. It looked like someone had neatly painted the whole thing with salt and pepper. The six coordinating chairs upholstered in red and black speckled vinyl surrounded it.

5 - The Living Room

The kitchen doorway led to our living room whose walls were ten feet high and tinted a deep sea green color. A white ceiling spilled down in a twelve-inch band, making it look rather like the lid of a gift box. Glossy white framework edged the doorways and windows. The four-feet-tall silver-painted radiator stood by the entrance to the back porch and bathroom.

The furnishings of our home ranged from antique to modern. Dad's black reclining vibrator chair and Mom's tan swivel rocker anchored the south wall like thrones for the king and queen of the house. What could be more fun than swivel rocking or vibrating? Such delights were pounced upon when our parents vacated the living room. A modern black pole lamp between them produced lighting in three directions for the ceiling and both chairs.

I got into a lot of trouble with Dad when I first learned how to sew. Not having a pin cushion, the chair's arm seemed an excellent place to corral my pins and needles. All would have been good and fine had I remembered to retrieve them when I abandoned the area. Dad came home one evening after a long hard day, so looking forward to relaxing in the comfort of the recliner. As he collapsed into the chair, his tired arms fell heavily on the armrests. A sharp awareness of pain followed. A shrill "Jilene!" decimated the anticipated quiet moment.

I snapped into fearful attention! A lesson on safety precautions unfolded in an outburst of controlled frustration. It did not help matters that we had recently been given our first game of jacks. The torture of walking barefoot on the pointy metal game pieces was too fresh in his mind. I am so sorry, Dad!

The long wall directly across from the kitchen was flanked with two tall windows dressed in white blinds and sheer curtains. Occasional gentle breezes caused the curtain sheers to swirl into the room. However, the curtain rods kept them from waltzing away. A lovely antique round pedestal table with a scrolled edge nestled between the rocker and the couch. A porcelain lamp graced its top on a white plastic doily. A large rectangular mirror centered between the windows reflected any welcomed light into the room. The couch rested beneath it.

Dad purchased a piece of cream-colored marble on one of his trips. He was rather handy; he framed it and added tapered legs to make a coffee table. Another time Dad came home with two statues of knights about two feet high made of stoneware. He converted them into lamps by drilling a hole in each base, attaching thin pipes, wiring them for light bulb sockets, and added lampshades. They flanked both ends of the couch.

A blonde-colored hi-fi stereo cabinet stood next to the window on the left side of the couch. A double-wide sliding door separated the living room from the front bedroom. The dark rosewood-colored console television cabinet rested on the other side. Thus our very eclectic living room was furnished.

One of my fondest memories happened in the living room. I was very young and had curled up on the couch with Dad to watch the television. There was a man who played the piano on a program every week. We listened quietly as each delicate note floated over the airways. I was totally dumbstruck with such incredible music! Dad noticed how quiet I was, and looking into my eyes; he saw tears gently falling down my cheeks. With the tenderness that matched the moment, he asked, "Jilene, why are you crying?"

The music caused an ache in my tiny heart. Overwhelmed, I could hardly speak. Finally, with an almost choked response, I said, "Daddy, it is so beautiful!"

He pulled me close to his chest and hugged me as if he could not let me go. That was one of the most tender moments I ever experienced.

6 - Housework and Loads of Laundry

Mom's domain was managing the house, the girls, and the rental properties. She was an excellent housekeeper. She kept the heavy wooden blinds on the windows dusted. At least once a year, she dismantled them and individually cleaned every slat. She scrubbed the floors on her hands and knees with Spic n Span® or Pine-sol®. Many women loved the scent of both cleaners, but I thought that they had a disagreeably strong odor. Between washings, armed with her trusty dust mop, she forever chased down "dust bunnies" that bred and hid under beds and furniture. She forbade the consumption of food outside the designated kitchen area.

Hours and hours were spent gathering the clothes, hauling them to the basement, and washing them in an old wringer washer. They did not have the spin dry function that washing machines have now. Each sopping wet piece was drug up from the tub and run through a set of rubber-coated rollers. In appearance, they looked like two pastry rolling pins placed close together. If not handled with care, one's fingers, hands, arms, or long hair were painfully entrapped by the rollers. Mom used bobby pins, and a scarf tied neatly over her hair when doing the laundry and other housework to avoid accidents. When the clothes went through the wringer the first time, she rinsed them through two more tubs of clean water. The wringing process was repeated after rinsing the clothes in clean water two more times. After the third wringing, she shook the clothes out, neatly placed them in the laundry basket, and lugged them to the back yard.

Mom hung her laundry on clotheslines with both scientific and artistic care. Like many other women, she was very organized. All like items hung together. The fourth clothesline closest to the fence was used first. Every item was sorted and hung by color and size. One clothespin was placed at the left corner of the first item. The next piece of clothing was placed over the right edge of the previous one. The second clothespin held them together. The process continued until the line was filled with no gap at all. It was a pretty clever method as it took half the number of clothespins to do the job. She gained two benefits from this method. More line was available, and the clothes did not slide around on windy days.

When the laundry was dry, Mom systematically pulled each piece off of the clothesline, folded it, and put it in the basket. Sheets and pillowcases smelled heavenly. I am not kidding! I am sure that the very act of breathing in the scent of laundry fresh off the line is most healthy.

Winter laundry hung on clotheslines strung in the basement. Bedsheets and other clothing often became stiff as a board when the weather was freezing. There was no heat in the basement. I remember sheets freeze-drying to the point that two people could carry them like pieces of framed art canvases. They made cracking sounds if you tried to fold them before they warmed up. Doing so also weakened the fabrics and sometimes caused tears.

It was a day of celebration when Mom got her modern agitating washer! The laundry chore graduated from the dark, dank basement next to the dirt floor where coal was once stored. The space between the refrigerator and sink in our kitchen was just the right spot. New laundry products, including powders, liquids, and solid laundry tablets, made their debut. The tablets rarely dissolved in the wash. One liquid detergent, in particular, gave us skin rashes.

Many companies added incentives to their cleaning product boxes or jars. Washcloths, dish towels, or glassware enticed customers to continue their purchases until their collections were complete. Mom collected a beautiful set of water and juice glasses. They were frosted and had black and silver maple leaf designs on them. Today I am the proud owner of those glasses and still have some of the boxes they came in.

Permanent press clothing was a thing for the future, and the new steam irons were not part of our lives yet. Almost all clothes were wrinkled and had to be ironed. Mom had a "sprinkling" bottle that she used to dampen the clothes before she ironed them. To streamline the job, she sprinkled and tightly rolled the dampened clothes into small bundles. Placing them in a large plastic zippered bag, she stored them in the refrigerator to keep them from drying out as she worked through the piles. She was spared the job of laundering and ironing Dad's shirts since he traveled so much until she got the new washer. Before then, the shirts were sent to a dry cleaner along with his suits. A delivery truck returned them hung neatly on hangers and wrapped in thin plastic covers.

Mom did her ironing either in the kitchen by the stove or in the big bedroom toward the front of the house. Sometimes she did her ironing in the living room where the airflow was much better and cooler. She hung the clothes in the door track of the double-wide sliding wooden door and later transferred them to the proper closets.

One day she was late getting the ironed clothes put away, so Dad's shirts were left hanging on the door track. My bed was across from that doorway. In the middle of the night, I woke up facing those huge white shirts about six feet from me. It was a breezy evening, and the moonlight gave the fluttering shirts the appearance of ghosts floating in the air. I was so terrified that when I finally caught my breath, I started screaming! It dawned on me what they were, and I was finally able to go back to sleep. I am sure that a new cartoon show called *Casper the Friendly Ghost* and other popular scary television shows like *The Twilight Zone, The Alfred Hitchcock Hour*, and *The Outer Limits* influenced the frightening experience.

7 - Mostly Marvelous Meals

Mom's meals were mostly marvelous but sometimes less than luscious. Breakfast was often the example of the latter and appeared to be the one of which she had the least interest. I watched her make eggs sunny side up in her cast iron skillet by flicking heated lard over them with her egg turner. Getting past that was hard. Dad seemed to enjoy them with coffee and canned biscuits, butter, honey, and bacon or spicy sausage. She made oatmeal or soggy cornflakes for us. The days when she served cream of wheat were much happier. Eventually, she worked her way into making French toast, American fried potatoes with onions, scrambled eggs, and store-bought honey buns with melted butter. Now that was much more enticing.

I hated breakfast so much I would try to skip it until the good Dr. Davis told Mom to make raw egg shakes for me. I decided to put up with soggy cornflakes rather than drink slimy raw eggs mixed with milk, sugar, and vanilla. I dreaded any form of breakfast eggs.

On the other hand, Mom excelled in making evening meals. When she cooked fantastic foods that we all enjoyed, no one was late to the table. Her baked macaroni and cheese was unbelievably delicious. It was made in layers with elbow macaroni noodles, milk, butter, and sliced Cracker Barrel® Sharp Cheddar cheese, salt, and pepper. Broccoli and cube steaks rounded out the meal. Cabbage rolls or meatloaf cozied up to scalloped potatoes and spinach. The spaghetti sauce simmered all day long, and it tasted even better on the second day. Believe it or not, I enjoyed Mom's making liver and onions. It is something that I will never be able to bring myself to make on my own! She made salmon patties, and her meatloaf patties were mouth-watering.

None of us liked the homemade chili, and I would have done anything rather than eat stewed tomatoes. When we were old enough, Terri and I did the dishes. On chili nights, we drug eating out to the point that our parents left the table. One of us stood guard at the kitchen door while the other tried to smash the chili down the drain. That was a little hard to do without a garbage disposal. The chili would have been much better without those stewed tomatoes in it!

We never ate rice or chipped beef at home. While Dad had been in the United States Navy during World War II and the Korean Conflict, those items had been a mainstay in the ship's galley. Thus he forbade their entry onto the table when he was present, though Mom snuck some rice into her meatloaf and cabbage rolls to make them stretch.

Nothing exceeded the perfection of her pot roast! A chuck roast covered with potatoes, carrots, broccoli, cabbage, and onions slow cooked in an electric pan for about four or five hours. Her mashed potatoes were a work of art. They sat in the serving bowl like a fluffy mountain. A big dollop of butter set on the top threatened to run down its sides like the lava flow of a volcano. She made terrific gravy to go with them. It still makes my mouth water and my nose search for that scent—hot and salty and comforting! Yum, yum! It was the meal I always requested for my birthday.

My two favorite birthday cakes were chocolate fudge and coconut. Mom always used cake mixes from Duncan Hines® or Betty Crocker®. Dad's favorite was pineapple upside-down cake.

However, her carrot cakes were made from scratch and incredibly delicious! Dad bought Mom a special grater made of metal, which stood on three legs. Being quite enthusiastic about the contraption, she filled it with carrot chunks and turned a crank to grate them into a large bowl. Then, she added pecans or walnuts and raisins to the batter, filled the cake pans, and popped them into the oven. While the cake baked, she made a delicious cream cheese frosting. The completed dessert was sprinkled with a layer of finely chopped nuts. The only reason you wanted to swallow the first bite was to get more. To me, it was the best dessert this side of heaven!

Mom also liked to make baked cinnamon apples, homemade fudge, and coconut bonbons. With the invention of prepackaged, refrigerated cookie dough, the term "homemade cookies" left our family. She tried making pies, but even she said that was a disaster as they always turned out like a sweet soup in a pie crust. If Dad wanted a pie bad enough, he usually bought pre-made mini pies. He liked to heat them in a frying pan.

In the summer, we drank iced tea or Mom's fruit punch. She got out her gallon-sized Tupperware® jug. Cans of lemonade and orange juice and a small bottle of grape juice were mixed with water and ice. The concoction was an ugly pink color but very refreshing. Sometimes she made Kool-aid®. When Dad was home, he lined us girls up at night to drink milk before we went to bed. He tried to get us to hurry by telling us with a certain sense of glee that, "It would put hair on our chests!" We were too young not to think that would be a good idea and made haste to win his approval.

When Dad was on the road for work, Mom's cooking was less of a grand production. Canned ravioli, canned soup, and sandwiches of ham, braunschweiger, bologna, or tuna were our fare. Sometimes sandwiches of egg salad, bacon, lettuce, and tomato, or peanut butter and jelly were served.

Many of these items were purchased across the street at Pete's Grocery. Getting there was a bit of a trick. The intersection of Page Boulevard (a four-lane highway) and Delaware Avenue had neither crosswalks nor traffic signals. Mom, being a veteran at crossing busy streets since her childhood, was up for the challenge. We stood at the edge of the street in front of our house, holding Mom's hands. As soon as there was a break in the traffic, she quickly escorted us to the double lines in the center of the road. We most often had to perch there because the intersection was built on a rise in the road, and if vehicles traveling from the east were short, they were not visible until they reached that point. We stood very tall and still and thinking ourselves to be as thin as possible until that traffic passed us. Then we very quickly and safely made it to the small parking area. That either worked up our appetites and or scared the desire to eat from us.

Anyway, we made it to the wood-framed building that shared one wall with the tavern on the corner. A tingling bell at the entrance announced customers as they came through. Nearly everything for food and cleaning supplies was displayed on the shelves of this store that was probably as old as our house. A butcher's case was in the back. Pete waited on each customer and pulled their selections from behind the sliding glass doors with great care. He cut all the meat, including the deli and cheese items, placed them on dark mauve-colored pieces of butcher paper, weighed and wrapped them tightly. He then took a grease pencil and marked the price and the contents on each package. He was very friendly and cheerfully treated each customer with great respect. He often knew, ahead of their requests, what they were going to order.

A huge jar of dill pickles rested on top of the meat case. Pete wrapped them the same way as he did the meats and cheeses, only adding a white hotdog shaped paper tray to keep the pickle juice from soaking the butcher paper. Mom often got a few to make pickle and mayonnaise sandwiches with Wonder Bread® for us. They were so cold and delicious.

Mom always had her purchases double-bagged at the register to ensure they would not fall apart while making the return trip across the street. We then returned to battle the traffic and made our way back to the house. If nothing else, the experience helped to teach us patience.

In the 1960s, we walked to the grocery store, half a block east of the house, and picked out our own pre-made "TV" dinners. They were packed in aluminum sectioned trays. Straight from the freezer to the oven to the table was the idea. I chose salisbury steak, roast beef, or turkey.

Prepackaged popcorn in aluminum cooking pan hit the store shelves. Jiffy-pop® attempted to make the preparation less of a mess. The popcorn was hard to cook without burning. Some companies promoted their jellies in collectible glassware. Someone invented a combination of peanut butter and jelly together in a swirled but identifiable mixture. I do not think that made the big time food list. It did not taste very good.

Holiday meals were kept only to our immediate family, which was sad but a feast nonetheless. For Thanksgiving, we almost always had a large turkey with homemade sausage stuffing. Homemade cranberry salad, green bean casserole, candied yams, mashed potatoes, and store-bought heat and eat rolls completed the meal. Pumpkin and mincemeat pies were our desserts, although Mom was the only one who ate the mincemeat. Christmas meal was usually the roast beef dinner or ham. Dad participated in a strange New Year's Eve custom. He felt that eating pickled herring and black-eyed peas brought good luck for the New Year. I never could get into that much, but to him, it was a great treat!

8 - Mealtime Strategies

The table was the family gathering area, especially when Dad was home. In school, we learned to pray before our meals, which then became our new custom. Mom insisted that we all eat together at the table at dinner time and on the weekends, which was a very good thing. However, there was a persistent conflict with Dad. Sometimes Mom won the battle, sometimes not.

Dad had a challenge with television and without hesitation, turned into "the king of the castle" when a favorite program was aired. We lived prior to the luxury of recording for the future. So viewers easily became captured prisoners for the duration.

If a program's time slot matched dinner, Dad drug the big console television set across the living room floor and placed it in the kitchen doorway. Not only did the prominent guest block the exit, but its place at the corner of the table was practically underneath Mom's right arm. Dad sat at the opposite end with a clear view of the screen. The daughters filled the seating in between. Conversation was relegated only to the commercial interruptions and "spit out" like ammunition with barely a sense of being heard before the program resumed. Unfortunately, this practice did much to stifle my ability to communicate. I feared not being able to make a point with everyone vying for attention.

The concept of the viewer controlled pause was in the far distant future. Many an evening, Mom would quietly fume over the ordeal. She really wanted dinner to be a time for family communication. I think the females in the family would have totally agreed. Dad's choices of entertainment mainly included programs of which the rest of us were not particularly fond. *The Honeymooners* was about an obnoxious man and his wife and their neighbors. *Rawhide* recounted the days of cattle drives in the old west. *Hee-Haw*, a country comedy-variety program, was full of all kinds of silliness. We did like *Car 54, Where are You?* which was a comedy about two police officers in a patrol car. After the program and dinner ended, Dad removed the "guest of honor" to its more natural habitat in the living room corner. He kept it company while the rest of us attended to the cleanup details.

On one of the evenings, when Mom won the communication battle, we enjoyed the meal and talked to each other. At some point in the conversation, Mom and Dad attempted to talk about something they were trying to keep us from perceiving. Thinking themselves very clever, they decided to spell words in reverse order. This became a standard method of diversion during several meals. It was not long before I began to decipher the code. Even though the letters raced through the air past my ears, it eventually dawned on me what was being said. I spouted off, "Ice cream!!!" with tremendous glee. They looked at each other and chuckled, realizing their chosen weapon of warfare was dismantled. Never again did they try that strategy. Ice cream always meant a trip to Velvet Freeze®, Dairy Queen®, or one of the other two local ice cream shops for a delicious treat.

Up and Above

9 – The Charm of the Rentals

*H*ighly motivated, Dad and Mom embraced the lives as landlord and lady. The income provided for the mortgage payments, management, and upkeep of the property. Mom dutifully managed the business end of the rentals, including housekeeping. Dad maintained the upkeep and repairs as needed.

Prior to their purchasing the property, the carriage house in the back was converted into a mechanic's garage. It accommodated space for servicing two vehicles, an office, and a private bathroom. The tenant was a nice man named Floyd. He happily provided service for cars for many of the locals.

The apartments in the main house were accessed through the front door and the hallway stairs to the right. The turning post at the first landing became a sort of mail ledge for the tenants. It stood about five feet tall with a flat square ledge on top. In our later childhood, it became the post office to our "mail clerk jobs." We dispatched the mail to the post for the tenants or to the kitchen table for our parents. I remember thinking about what an important job it was to make those deliveries.

The staircase to the second floor was intriguing. At the age of four, it beckoned for my attention. With the first unsupervised opportunity, I enthusiastically scrambled its height. Losing my balance at the top, I tumbled with greater speed and crashed on the landing on the first floor. A good lecture about a healthy respect for the stairs was the reward for my curiosity. The scar from a small gash over my left brow testifies to a not-so-triumphant adventure!

The second story of the house fanned out into three separate apartments. Each was furnished with a double bed, an armoire for clothing, an easy chair, a side table, and a lamp. The living areas had floral wallpaper and coordinating linoleum flooring. An oversized wooden door separated the front apartment from its nearest neighbor. It remained locked and blocked by the armoires. Each apartment included its own private sunny kitchen with a window, a porcelain sink, an old refrigerator, a gas stove, and a small dinette set.

The two apartments toward the back of the house were dimly lit and ventilated by single windows. In contrast, the front apartment was bright and airy with its three windows. It was my favorite of all the spaces in the house. It had an especially homey feeling and a perfect view of the front yard. I imagined sitting there contentedly gazing out the windows at the end of the long summer afternoons but never got the chance.

I was always drawn to rooms bathed in natural sunlight. Somehow they emitted such a feeling of a warm welcome. In contrast, Mom was more than content to keep curtains drawn. She felt the rooms would stay cooler. She did, on occasion, complain that the light bothered her eyes. Yet, the darkness gave me a sense of unexplained sadness.

The second-floor apartments shared a bathroom to the right of the staircase. On rare occasions, Mom gave the old white clawfoot bathtub a thorough scrubbing and let us take our baths up there. That was only when all the tenants were away from the house so that we would not inconvenience them. It was a special treat. I felt like a princess when I had that bathroom all to myself! The sunlight and breeze filtered through the neighbors' trees and the window. It was quite pleasant and much better than our bathroom connected to the back porch on the first floor.

A door to the left of the front apartment hid a staircase to the attic studio-like apartment. It was very spacious, covering the entire length and width of the house. The charming dormer windows were centered on each of the four sides of the attic. One was hidden in the bathroom on the western wall. A kitchen was nestled in the southwest corner. Access to a sun porch was through the rear next to the kitchen. All the walls on that floor were pink.

10 – Among the Tenants

Since there was no separate office space in our house, the kitchen table became the front desk. Tenants met with Mom to sign rental agreements, make payments, and discuss any problems that needed attention. She took out her receipt book with the carbon paper to make copies of the transactions. If there was a particularly positive relationship with the tenant, she offered them tea or coffee, and they would sit and chat for a while. Most of the tenants were good people, and some remained longtime friends.

The attic was rented for a few years by some brothers and a friend of theirs. Mom was apprehensive at first and laid down the rules carefully to them. When she saw their respectfulness and sincerity, she formalized their rental agreement. They were from farms in Nebraska and were all young men of fine character. They became good family friends who participated in several holiday celebrations. The friend's name was Ron, but everyone called him Peanuts. The brothers' names were Gene and Marvin.

They invited us to their families' farms in Nebraska one year for Thanksgiving. Both families were so kind and could not do enough to make us feel more welcomed.

The men took Dad with them to hunt for pheasant for dinner. They got a huge one and brought it home to be dressed and cooked. I had never seen a pheasant before, and I had never eaten anything I had seen with its feathers or fur. That was quite an experience for me. The mother put that bird in a pan, sat it on her lap, and feathers flew as she plucked them. Being a city girl brought up on grocery store food, I was amazed and a little scared at the sight. Once I got over the shock of it all, I thoroughly enjoyed the meat.

The next morning, we were invited for breakfast at Gene and Marvin's family home. We met their sister, and she was just as friendly as her brothers. They had the largest table I had seen to that point. It was filled with all sorts of fantastic melt-in-your-mouth breakfast delights. Fresh milk, hand-churned butter, homemade biscuits with preserves and jellies were among the many treats set before us. Several hours later, we were on our way home, but we kept in touch with both families for many years.

Marvin and Ron joined the service. Gene also left. Ron returned when he completed his duty and married his sweetheart. They found a place in St. Louis.

We were invited to their apartment for dinner one evening. Ron was very tall and handsome, and his wife, Mary, was beautiful and thin. She wore a stylish black dress with a full skirt. Mom had us wear dresses and bought little wired bracelets strung with pearls for us to wear for the occasion.

Mary made spaghetti, but it did not taste the same as Mom's did. We were told that we needed to eat it anyway and to be polite. The room was filled with laughter as the young couple shared the stories of their early days of marriage. It was easy to see that they loved each other very much.

Another lady named Edna lived in the front apartment for quite a while. She was a lot of fun. She worked at Chuck-a-burger and wore a cute uniform with an apron and cap. She always smelled like hamburgers, which was pretty neat. The scent made me want to go out to eat. Sometimes she brought home some cola syrup and gave it to Mom, who used it for cough medicine for us. Edna married and moved on. When she had her first baby, we were invited to her house. She served iced tea with fresh mint leaves from her backyard.

There was one father who had a teenage daughter. She had one of those poodle skirts and an angora sweater, which were so popular in the 50s. Almost every day after school, she came to our floor to watch American Bandstand with us. Her visits made us feel a little like she was an older sister for a short time. She attended Wellston High School several blocks north of our house. Along with Gene and Peanuts, she and her father loved being a part of our family activities.

The Ways of Our Family

11 - "*Lights, Action, Camera!*"

*I*n 1957, television commercials touted the new 8mm home movie camera. Many a situation comedy displayed family friends lounging in mock living room scenes. A host fumbled with a portable viewing screen and loaded the newest release into a projector while the hostess attended to the refreshments and the comfort of the guests.

At last, the moment arrived, the room darkened, and moving pictures provided a visual feast. The silence of the film was countered by the commentaries of the family and a great variety of responses from the guests.

Sometimes, the films transported viewers to distant lands and exciting vacations. Other times, films of family events recorded heartwarming memories and brought laughter and melancholy. Every theme portrayed gave the illusion that anyone could produce their own films. Thus, a home movie camera became the latest modern convenience that "no home should be without."

That encouragement was all that was needed. Dad surveyed our family situation. Two young girls were growing up quickly. His imagination skimmed through future memories that could be lost if not captured. The bug had bitten.

Soon he came home sporting his new "toy," an 8mm home movie camera. Over the next few weeks, he gathered all the paraphernalia that supports the venture. Armed and ready, our personal producer, director, and cameraman was now in pursuit of a good story.

Opportunities to put his gear into "action" soon arrived, and we were off to fill up reel upon reel of film. Over the next twelve years or so, many special activities made it into the collection of recorded memories.

The first movie made included a visit from two of the tenants from the attic, Gene and "Peanuts." Peanuts brought his girlfriend and the three of them met with us in the living room.

Mom, recently, had a portrait made of herself, Terri, and me as Dad's Father's Day present. She was quite proud of it, so the oohing and aahing of the gift with the family and friends had to be captured on film.

Next, records were stacked on the stereo, and our living room became a small dance hall. Dad and Mom started "jitterbugging" to favorite dance tunes. Gene and Peanuts took turns dancing with Mary and manning the camera. Before I knew it, Dad picked me up, Mom held Terri, and the four of us had a merry time dancing.

The first beautiful heavy snowfall that winter brought with it a great occasion. The making of a snowman and a terrific snowball fight in the front yard was in order. The sun shone brightly in a cloudless blue sky on that crisp icy day. Dad got busy rolling three huge snowballs for the snowman's body. Terri and I "helped" him carry them to just the right spot in the yard. Mom buzzed by to round out some edges. When Mr. Snowman's head was in place, Dad bedecked him temporarily with his black hat and pipe. The "new family member" was then complete. We had less than a minute to admire the creation when the snowball fight heightened into a frenzy. Peanuts and Gene joined the action along with the teenage girl and her dad from the second floor. Laughter and screaming filled the air. With little time to pack the snow into balls, the attackers hurled great chunks of snow. A few times, the ladies were heavily bombarded but were not easily defeated. Mom's glasses went flying, and at one point, Dad was hit hard enough that he bit down hard on his pipe and broke it in two. All in all, it was a splendid time carefully captured in brilliant color on three rolls of Kodachrome® film.

The snow soon melted, and spring ushered in the Easter season before us. Two little girls carrying colorful baskets excitedly hunted for eggs in the front yard. Terri wore the beautiful orchid and white-dotted swiss dress with puffed sleeves and a white collar. (It was the same dress which I wore in the pre-mentioned portrait. Mom had the studio change it to a light blue to better coordinate with Terri's red dotted swiss and Mom's tan dress.) My Easter dress that year was the color of a cantaloupe. It had puffed sleeves and a chocolate brown split overskirt and bodice. Mom loved to have us wear very full slips underneath to make the skirts of the dresses stick out as far as possible.

Our friends from upstairs joined in. Glimpses of waving passersby were caught on film. Dad showed off the family in front of his current new car, a 1958 two-door Chevrolet Belair in Cay Coral and Arctic White. It was pretty sharp looking with its four headlights and four front directional lights. Candy from the baskets was shared with all.

The third occasion recorded was a summer visit from Dad's sister, our Aunt Kay, and her family. Uncle Cal and cousins Patty, Barbara, and Jimmy, became fine extras for the front yard games. We played ring around the rosie, tag, and chase. Riding the little red tricycle and our yellow AMF V8 Pacesetter Convertible pedal car also provided some action. The men had to show off their strength by picking up the wives and carrying them toward the camera. Uncle Cal playfully paddled Patty for chasing her mom and yanking on her skirt. Jimmy, completely outnumbered by the female children, held his own in the film with a big smile. Patty and Barbara showed off their cartwheel skills.

So went the first year and a half of home movies. Many more adventures lay ahead.

12 - Dad and His Daughters

"Daddy and the daughters' times" were always fertile ground for memorable experiences. We greatly anticipated running errands or taking those special trips as we loved being the center of his attention, and there was rarely a dull moment.

When my sister, Terri, was about three and a half, and I was five, we were awakened before the sun was up. Mom dressed us, and we followed Dad out the front door. He was carrying a box and long poles, which he loaded into the car. Soon we found out that we were going on a fishing trip, whatever that was. We drove for hours and wound up at some stream. Evidently, Dad's buddies were going fishing, and he decided to share the experience with us. Pulling into the parking area, we saw several other men armed with boxes and fishing poles. They were laughing, and Dad seemed very excited to join them. Jumping out of the car, Terri and I were drinking in the obvious elation of the group. Dad mentioned something about staying close, and off we headed to the stream.

I remember the sky being a beautiful blue with lots of white clouds. The sun reflected on the rippling waves like thousands of sparkling diamonds. We were drawn to this new adventure like bees to the pollen of brightly colored flowers. Along the water's edge were clumps of grass nearly as tall as we were. We happily flitted from one to the next, eager to see what might appear. Spotting something gleaming very close to the water's edge, I screamed out in great delight! "Daddy, Daddy! Look at the big fat worm!!!"

Like a knight in shining armor, he came charging toward us, to rescue his damsels in distress! He cautiously but quickly pulled his fair little maidens away from a big silver-colored snake to safety. Then, he firmly reminded us to stay close to him. We did not realize that we could be in danger, but we were happy to be with Dad.

The morning moved along, and the men fished and chatted and watched Dad and his two daughters. It began to get pretty hot, so the entire group crossed over the stream to a spot with more shade. We all settled in nicely, and the fishing continued. It was not long before the bright sunlight was completely blocked by summer clouds, and a torrential rain shower drenched us all in the process!

To the total amazement of the entire group of men, I began fuming and stomping and going off on Dad. The contents of my sheer and utter frustration filled their ears as I adamantly stated, "This was the stupidest thing I had   ever seen in my entire life!!! Here we are on this side of the stream getting soaking wet, and our car is on the other side!!! How could Daddy be so stupid???"

Dad was totally dumbfounded! He could not keep from giggling along with the guarded laughter of his friends as his little girl spouted off her assessment of the situation at the grand old age of five. Looking back, I know that I should have received a good smack on the behind, followed by a lesson in respect. Dad, however, enjoyed the moment and element of flabbergasted surprise. Another gem was added to the collection of the tales of his relationships with his little daughters.

There was a shopping incident that involved a large parking lot. It was probably built on a twenty-degree slope. The weather was quite cold, and Dad anticipated his time in the store to be quick, so he decided to leave us in the car for the duration. Before he left, he told us that he would be just a few minutes, keep the doors locked, and not unlock the car for anyone.

As he disappeared through the entrance of an establishment, we started exploring the mechanics of the the vehicle's interior. I do not remember which one of us decided to pretend that we were driving. The steering wheel was grabbed and remembering seeing Dad move that stick attached to it; the shift was moved into neutral. We were without the slightest sense of accomplishment or realization that the car was rolling backwards.

Just then, God prompted several gallant strong men to race across the parking lot. They valiantly surrounded and halted the car. "Little girl, little girl! Unlock the door!" the man at the driver's window excitedly insisted. I am sure we did not realize the danger we were in, but we conveyed our dad's adamant instructions to him. "Our Daddy told us not to unlock the door for anyone!"

So being at an impasse, our rescuers steadily manned the sides of our carriage until the king could return for his princesses. Soon he did and was met with some stern words of rebuke! The man at the driver's window had to grin. Then he commended the king for his obedient daughters who refused to disobey their daddy. He realized there was no way we were going to give any rescuers access to the car. Dad was shaken. He carried the admonishment as well as the encouragement close to his heart, for he dearly loved his little girls.

On another day, Terri had a memorable encounter with Dad while he was making some house repairs. He laid out all the materials on the floor, cutting pipes and arranging them in order. She was right beside him like a shadow, fascinated with every detail. The job required the use of a butane torch to solder some pipes together. He lit it and set it aside. Trying to get closer to see what he was doing, Terri excitedly leaned in, accidentally knocking over the torch. Dad's pants caught fire, but he was able to get the flames out pretty quickly! I think it scared her more than it hurt him. I'm pretty sure she was devastated by the experience. All in all, I believe it bounded them even more closely together.

When I was a little girl, I had a fascination with music boxes. I had been able to see their inner workings and just knew Dad could make one for me. So with the faith of a child, I made my plea. I waited days in great anticipation of the tinkling notes that my very own music box would play. I knew it had to be perfect since Dad was making it, and he seemed excited for the challenge of delighting his eldest daughter. Then one night, I saw him in the kitchen with a large empty ham can from which he decided to make my music box. He snipped the can at both ends at the top edge and then attached a long stick. I wondered how this was going to be the highly anticipated beautiful music box for which I was longing. Then he started attaching strings that were left over from his guitar!?! Wait a minute, I thought, that does not look like the music box I wanted!

Dad was so proud as he worked on his version of a music box. Unfortunately, I was young and heartbroken. I had not learned how to be grateful or hide my disappointment. For me, at that time, two realizations occurred simultaneously. One, Dad did not have the slightest idea what a music box was and two, he was not perfect; in fact, he was very human! (Little girl devastation!!!)

I have no idea what happened to the "music box" or even if I ever played with it. I do know this: Dad loved me, and he tried to bless me. Love does not always bless according to our preconceived ideas. Love does bring beautiful memories of real human and imperfect people. I thank God, who is perfect and loves perfectly and for Daddy, who tried his best in his human way to love his daughter.

As with most families, disagreements between parents can become unbearable for the entire family. Our parents' marriage was often less than amicable. For some reason unknown to Terri and me, one such event rendered us without a family Christmas dinner. Dad was determined that the battle was not going to deprive his girls. He bundled the two of us up in our new fake fur tops and winter slacks, coats, and boots and escorted us to the car. It was an unusually dark evening not only in appearance but also in mood. Stores were closed. Lights that weeks before paraded the festivities of the season were black. For at least an hour, we searched the streets for the sign of a restaurant that was still open. Warm lights on a corner somewhere in the snow and slush-filled streets of downtown St. Louis beckoned us to a half-filled diner. The three of us were seated to enjoy the holiday meal. Our hearts were aching from the hurt of the previous outbursts of anger. Yet Dad was determined to provide for a nice and quiet turkey dinner and pumpkin pie for us. When pain so strong is unselfishly set aside to provide comfort for the innocent, it is a gift well worth being remembered with gratefulness. I am glad that Dad, by example, at that moment in time, instilled the priority of compassion for others over the pain to self.

New Adventure

13 - What Is Love?

*A*mazingly, most of us go through the day-to-day routines without really paying much attention. I guess there is a lot to be said for the status quo and the sense of security it brings. Then a deviation from the normal presents itself. All of a sudden, we wake up as if we are in a completely different world and are forced to become aware of untested waters. There can be no growth without change, as I heard one preacher oft repeat, "Constant change is here to stay!" Change happens, and children are definitely not exempt from it.

If my parents talked about God when my sister Terri and I were little, I do not remember it. Evidently, we were both Christened as infants. However, in those early years, our family remained nominal church attendees at best. Once I reached about the age of five, their hearts were tugged, and church began to be important.

One day in the week became different than the rest. It was Sunday. Dad wore his suit and hat, which was nothing new, but Mom was unusually decked out, donning a pretty dress, high heels, a fashionable hat, and gloves. She clothed us in what she called our "Sunday best" complete with fancier dresses, hats, patent leather shoes, and little purses.

Dad went to the car to prepare for the drive and wait for us. Mom made one last spot check and rushed us out the front door to meet him. In the car, we were both handed a coin or two, and a small envelope. We were told to put the coins into the envelopes and then into our purses.

More often than not, there seemed to be a little tension in the car over being late. Off we drove to Grace Lutheran Church on the western edge of downtown Wellston. The sturdy red brick building was built in 1910 and is still standing today². It was only about six or seven blocks from our house.

A strange new activity unfolded. We were rarely out of the company of at least one parent, but now our parents escorted us to a building separated from the church. We followed a concrete staircase to the basement, and they left us with some people we did not know. We had no clue where they went at the time.

The people they left us with were friendly enough. They asked our ages and accordingly separated us to different sections of the dimly lit room. We were told to sit on the cold, neatly arranged metal chairs. Each had a green book placed on the seat. I browsed through one and did not understand what it was. It had very few pictures but lots of straight lines with odd dots across them.

Soon, other children filled the seats, and a lady came to the front of the room. She had some papers and books and began saying something about prayer. I watched as everyone folded their hands, bowed their heads, and closed their eyes. Then the lady started talking as if to someone she could not see but was sure he was listening.

After that, they began to talk to us about God. They said something that caused most of the children to pick up those green books and flip through the pages. I found out they were called hymnals. Someone else played the piano from the corner of the room. In a matter of weeks, Terri and I learned to sing a song with as much confidence as the rest of the children. That song became a great foundation for my life:

"Jesus Loves Me"
Jesus loves me, this I know
For the Bible tells me so;
Little ones to Him belong;
They are weak, but He is strong.
Yes, Jesus loves me!
Yes, Jesus loves me!
Yes, Jesus loves me!
For the Bible tells me so!

At that point, I did not know who this Jesus was, but I thought that if He loves me even though I was little and He was strong, I was all in for that! Besides that, the song said three times that He loves me, and something called a Bible tells me so!

From that first week on, Terri and I learned more and more about God and Jesus through the stories they told us. We saw the praying, listened to the piano, and learned to sing the songs that were in the green book. We played a little and worked on some paper crafts. Then we learned some verses that we were told came from that Bible.

Before we left each week, we were given the opportunity to put those envelopes that our parents gave us into a basket that was passed around. Honestly, that put me in a bit of a dilemma. Each Sunday, our parents gave us the few coins to put in those envelopes, and now we were being asked to turn around and give them away? I was young but old enough to recognize that money was used to buy things. If I had money, I could buy things! That was when I was first introduced to sacrificial giving. At first, it stung a bit, but then the people told us many people did not know about God and Jesus. The money we gave would be used to bring them the news that they were loved, too! I was excited about being loved, and I thought it was a good idea that other people should find that out for themselves. So when the basket was passed each week, I began to think about how I felt about being loved and how more people would find out about that love. I started to get excited about the envelopes and looked forward to bringing them to the children's room each week.

14 – Grace Moves to Pagedale

Before the summer of 1958, Grace Lutheran Church moved to their new sanctuary at 1425 Ferguson Avenue in Pagedale. It was directly across the street from Concord Lutheran School. On the day of the dedication service, most of the congregation literally walked the little more than one mile together from the prior location on Easton Avenue. It was a fantastic experience and a grand celebration.

The new structure was built with light rust-colored bricks. A tall narrow roof covered the sanctuary with a basement below. A bell tower and a two-story educational wing with a basement flanked the north side.

Heavy wooden doors opened into the large welcoming narthex (entry area). Shelves and hooks were hung along the walls to place overcoats and the men's hats. To the north side of the area was a "cry" room where mothers could be with their infants and still view the service through a window. A wall of windows set with beautiful wooden doors for three entrances separated the narthex from the sanctuary. The windows could be opened when there was a need for overflow seating. Two rows of long wooden hickory nut-colored pews (benches) filled the large room. Racks attached to the back of the pews held bibles, navy-colored hymnals from the former church building, pencils, and envelopes. A few years later, new red

Lutheran Hymnals replaced the navy ones. Toward the front and on the left, an alcove pocketed a baptismal font for Christenings.

Two ornately carved pulpits stood at the front of the church. From there, the ministers shared the selected readings from the Bible and delivered sermons. The altar stood apart from the congregational area and was separated by a kneeling rail where congregants could pray and receive communion. A row of tall candles rested on the altar, and two candelabras stood beside each end. All candles were lit during the church services. Above and behind the altar, a very tall empty cross was embedded into a window of stained gemstone colored glass. The cross extended outside the the window frame and was also visible outside the building welcoming all who came in. It was a reminder that Jesus Christ died for our sins and indeed rose from the dead, sits at the right hand of God, is making prayers of intercession for us, and is preparing a place for us to be with Him. We were also taught that the Holy Spirit was with us to show us the things of God.

On the north and south walls of the sanctuary, nave windows made of stained glass portrayed scenes from the Bible, including the creation and the flood. The balcony over the narthex held the choir loft, and a grand pipe organ resonated the most unforgettable worship music when beautifully played. Initially, the place for the organ was built without leaving a space for the seating of the organist. It was redesigned so that the floor and railing jutted out nicely and appeared as if it had been part of the original design.

A large stained glass window was set in the back wall in a triangular space beneath the roof. It depicted symbols of the twelve apostles. God used their courage and sacrifice to bring us the message of His love and salvation. Seeing the window each week was a reminder to do the same.

Our family sat together in the services at Grace on Ferguson Avenue. Dad was one of the ushers who helped people find seats and collect the offering. He slipped in beside us when he was not actively ushering.

Sunday at church was a wonderful time for me, a time to get away from the world and feel close to God and hear His Word. Singing hymns drew me closer and closer to the feeling that I was loved. No matter what happened, I could know assuredly that He would never leave me nor forsake me. Memories of those Sundays in church and what I learned about God and His Word have carried me through my life in both the good and the bad times.

Note: On May 6th, 2018, I had the blessed privilege to return for the 60th Anniversary Celebration of the Ferguson Avenue, Pagedale location. It was there that I reviewed, with all attending, many memories of the church and the school. What a heart-warming and teary experience that was!

15 - Next Steps

Several weeks after being introduced to Sunday School, other new adventures were added to my weekday routine. Mom woke me earlier than usual and helped me put on a dress rather than the little one-piece playsuits I usually wore. She fixed my long hair, separating a squared section on the top, which she turned into a small ponytail. She always pulled the rubber band very tightly to keep my hair from falling into my face. (Ouch!) She rushed me to the breakfast table for a quick bowl of cereal and colorful aluminum glass filled with milk. With a quick kiss, she told me to wait for my father.

That first day of school, Dad grabbed my hand, and we walked across the street that was beside our house. We stood on that corner, beside the used car lot, and chatted as many parents and their young children do. I was excited, but I did not know why. His hand was huge over my tiny hand. That was comforting and reassuring. He had a smile that could warm any heart. He was dressed for work in his dark suit, white shirt and conservative tie, polished shoes, and hat. To me, he was the most handsome man in the world! Together we watched as a big yellow bus rolled toward us. Dad coaxed me gently onto the bus. Letting go of my lifeline, I climbed aboard and found a seat by the window, peering out in his direction. The door closed, and the driver pulled out. I saw a big smile on Dad's face, and he waved, I heard him calling out, "Bye, Sissie, have a nice day!" As we drove away, he became smaller and smaller until I could no longer see him. The sound of his voice left my ears and planted itself in my heart.

"Bye, Sissie! Have a nice day!"

After making the rounds to pick up the other students, we entered the school driveway and got off the bus. Someone directed us into the building and led me into the very first classroom inside the front doors. It was the kindergarten room with many children my age. The tables were arranged in a big squared C-shape to give good eye contact between the teacher and the students. Mrs. Ameiss introduced herself and took the roll. She seemed tall to me, and older than Mom, and she talked a lot.

I was very excited when she brought out a stack of small boxes with lids on them individualized with our names. Quite a production was made of this dispersal, and each child's face lit up with hearing their names called and seeing them printed on their new gift. It was as if we were receiving something as valuable as gold and gave us a sense of awe and responsibility. It was definitely no mundane procedure. When we were told to open the boxes, I felt like my whole world had opened up. I was impressed because I had never seen crayons before! Much to my delight, she gave us careful instructions to only use one crayon at a time and always place it back into the box before using another color. Those instructions were not only for organization but also to keep them from rolling off our tables and breaking on the floor. After each session of using our crayons, Mrs. Ameiss carefully picked up the boxes from her students and stored them until the next event for their use occurred.

One day we were required to bring in a shirt for art projects. One of Dad's old shirts was enlisted for the task. That was very funny to me as Dad's shirt practically swallowed me! At that time, I was introduced to finger paints. After becoming a seasoned artist at school, Mom decided to get some paint for me to use at home. She invested in one bottle—one color—green! Because of the big influence that Walt Disney had on children at the time, I was exposed to fairies and princesses, and of course, I believed that everyone should be wearing crowns and carrying wands. I dove into my picture with gusto! Imagination was intensely required with the use of only my solo grass green. I thought and thought and carefully laid my paper out in landscape fashion in front of me and loaded my fingers with the paint. Up and down, up and down I painted, all the way across my "canvas." I proudly showed Mom my creation. "What is it?" she asked.

I could not believe I had to tell her! "That is Daddy, that is you, that is me, and that is Terri, and we all have crowns and wands!" I guess it was hard to see everyone behind the tall grass in my picture!

I learned my ABCs and 123s and how to spell my name in kindergarten. For some reason, my parents did not see a need to teach me those things and must have felt that it was the school's responsibility. I was glad to learn them. I also was drenched in the social skills of being around children my age, which was still pretty new to me. The only other time that had happened was the recent addition of Sunday School life. Friendship was a new word I wanted to learn.

At the end of one of the exciting days in school, we were dismissed as usual to head for the buses to go home. I hurriedly found my new friend and piled into the seat next to her. We giggled and chatted and tried to teach each other new clapping games that were the rage for all the little girls of the day to pass the time on the long ride home.

(I need to divert here a little and give some background. I was the third smallest girl in my class. I was a very fair, blue-eyed, dishwater blonde haired (according to my mother), scrawny little girl. On top of that, my ears stuck out. I had a love for dark eyes and dark hair because of Mom, and it was fueled by watching the breathtakingly beautiful Loretta Young on television every afternoon as she all but floated gracefully into the living room set in the most elegant of gowns to give the prelude to her television drama show.)

Now, my friend and her older sister were two of the prettiest girls I had ever seen. They had gorgeous, thick, dark, curly hair and big brown eyes. My friend was not much bigger than I was. Her sister and another girl sat behind us. The sister jumped into the middle of our game, and with the confident air of a wise prophet, enthusiastically inquired if I knew how to save a seat on the bus. With all the excitement of an avid disciple, I longed for the information that was about to be broadcast to my ears. I listened carefully as she unfolded the great mystery. All I had to do was take a crayon and write my name in big letters on the back of the seat in front of me. With great fervency, I wielded my carefully chosen instrument of inscription, which she supplied. Then with whole-hearted commitment, I brandished my name, which I had just learned to write on the rough textured aluminum back of the seat in front of me! What delight filled my heart as I realized that this was now my very own place on the bus, and I would not have to scramble to find a seat again! What a kind thing it was for my friend's big sister to share this vital information with me!

The next day, I could not wait until school was over! Even though I knew my seat was already saved, I made my way as quickly as possible to the bus. I would have run, but we were not allowed to run in the halls. I climbed the steps of the bus and proudly approached my reserved seat. The atmosphere was filled with excited chatter as students filled the other seats. Then, just before the door was about to close, two big men came aboard. Even though I was a novice in the school, I knew who the principal and the eighth-grade teacher were. The principal was a very tall man who had the carriage of Abraham Lincoln, and the eighth-grade teacher had a crew cut and also carried an air of absolute authority. The bus got quiet enough to hear a pin drop. Then the principal asked, "Who is Jilene?" Wow! I was so excited! With a big smile on my face, I stood up and acknowledged that I was Jilene! I was elated when he asked me to get my things and come to the front of the bus. That quickly changed when I found myself on the way to the principal's office, where the moment of pride and exhilaration turned into fear and devastation. I do not remember much that happened after that, but it was made very clear to me that it was not acceptable to write my name on the back of the seat on a bus. I became so afraid after that experience that my heart would pound if I even saw the principal or the eighth-grade teacher. My heart was broken to find out that my friend's sister would so delightfully lead me into the misguided path of graffiti. I wanted to trust her so much. That event at the age of five haunted my life in elementary school.

16 – The Walls Are Alive

*E*ver-changing life goes on, and every new encounter becomes another link in the chain of experience. Church, Sunday School, and school were not the only new changes in our lives.

Since there was only one large bedroom for two adults and two little girls, my parents decided to convert the good-sized porch at the back of the house into a bedroom for themselves. They were so excited about the process. Dad insulated the room and finished the walls with decorative knotty pine boards leaving the windows intact. Access to the backyard was through that room, and a closet was positioned directly across from the back door. The entrance to the bathroom was next to the closet. This gave ample opportunity for watching the progress of the project, a matter of no uncertain consequence. So whether we were going to the back yard to play or to the bathroom, Terri and I had to be very careful during the renovation process.

Dad remodeled the bathroom at the same time, replacing the long ago worn out metal shower stall. That was an excellent thing for him to do. I remember the extremely gross feeling of the crumbly wet rusted metal of the shower floor on my feet. It still turns my stomach a little to think of standing on it.

The sink and toilet were in good shape, so no changes were needed there. A small window gave good light and ample ventilation. If it was necessary for a person to park there for an extended visit, there was often a cool breeze and a delightful view of the next-door neighbor's backyard.

Dad put some tile on the floor and finished the small linen closet next to the shower. With the installation of the stained hollow core doors to the bathroom and the bedroom closet, the project was nearing its completion. For some reason, Dad was not concerned about installing doorknobs on the doors to the bathroom or their closet, so we learned to open them by scooching our little fingers between them and the door frames.

With the installation of window shades and sheer curtains completed, Mom finished her last project before they moved into the room. She picked out a warm pink paint color for the remaining walls and went to work with great pride.

The paint dried, and they moved their blond bed and chest of drawers into the room. Mom laid a dresser scarf of woven stripes in bright colors on the top of the dresser. A small carved jewelry box sat on its center. Both of those items were purchased while Dad was stationed in San Diego, California, with the Navy during the early days of their marriage. With the linens laid out, the bed was dressed, and that evening they moved into their new private haven away from the little girls in the front room of the house.

I was so excited for them. Days passed while I thought and thought with great contemplation as to what I could do to put a final touch on their special place. I became keenly aware that they had no artwork on their beautiful, warm pink walls. With my vivid imagination sparked by a recent trip to the St. Louis Zoo and the advanced art skills I had developed in my kindergarten career, I determined that a rendition of the tallest giraffes I could muster would be the pièce de résistance.

Armed with no more than a lead pencil and great enthusiasm, I proceeded to turn my vision into reality, carefully rendering each stroke on the chosen wall while Dad was at work, and Mom was preoccupied elsewhere in the house. A very handsome Daddy giraffe was drawn as tall as I could make him, and a gorgeous smaller Mommy giraffe stood close by. Of course, two beautiful little girl giraffes completed the delightful scene. I stepped back and admired my work with great pride!

I could not wait for Dad to get home, and I prodded Mom to go to the bedroom for the unveiling! I had the biggest smile on my face! She took one look and started screaming. As you can probably guess, it was not the cry of joy and delight that I had anticipated, it was the agony of shock and distress over the ruination of her newly painted walls!

The anticipation of a huge smile on Dad's face that I had expected as a result of my gift to them turned to fear of what was going to happen to me when he got home. The never-changing maternal statement of, "Wait until your father comes home!" rang out with all its might, and the fear that accompanies such a statement mounted.

Eventually, Dad did arrive, and as has often happened in my life, the stress of the situation left me without a memory of what exactly transpired at that moment. All in all, neither of my parents had the enthusiasm for my artwork for which I had hoped. The results of the event did reap the following foundational principles for my life: First of all, join in on the excitement your parents have for their projects; secondly, the never-changing paternal statement was unbendingly applied, "Look with your eyes and not with your hands!"; finally, never, never, never, never draw on walls (or bus seats for that matter)!

Well, I guess the statement that many great artists are not appreciated until their demise applied to me. I wonder if this event subversively prompted Dad never to let me sign up for art classes in my later school years. Pity, I could have made a fabulous animal artist! Maybe I should have asked for their permission.

17 - Dad's Big Surprise

*I*n May of 1959, I turned six years old. Dad had been out of town all week, and he came to pick us up at the church one late afternoon. Bearing a twinkle in his eye and a smile from ear to ear, he rushed into the fellowship hall and pulled Mom aside to talk for a moment. He then turned to Terri and me and enthusiastically said, "Hurry, girls, let's get in the car!" Without sharing any details of what was happening, he took us to the St. Louis Arena where the air was filled with lights, laughter, and the sounds of heralding music calling people through the front doors! We could not believe our eyes as Dad escorted us through the crowds, passing row by row of seats amidst the cries of, "Popcorn, peanuts, Cracker Jacks!" Here a clown, there a clown, everywhere we looked, clowns in bright costumes and garish faces peppered the Arena! Before we knew it, Dad was leading us into a ringside box seat section. His chest was about to explode at the thought of where he was taking us. I could feel my heart pounding as it was just beginning to dawn on us that we were at the circus, an event I never dreamed I was going to see!

It turned out that the Seventy-Seventh Annual St. Louis Police Circus was being held at the Arena just at the time of my birthday. Somehow Dad got tickets for the event and was totally able to hide the surprise from his daughters. We were ecstatic!

Moments later, the clamoring music became more organized as the lights dimmed. A spotlight pointed out the ringmaster, and he cried out the familiar line we had heard from episodes of circuses on television. "LADIES AND GENTLEMEN. . . !"

Terri and I could hardly breathe, trying to gather in all the sights and sounds and smells. The circus parade began, and a preview of all the acts of the evening danced before our eyes, not twenty or thirty feet from our reach! We watched all that was set before us in total amazement! As was promised, the performers made their way to their perspective places and delighted us with various acts.

Among the feast of amusements were tightrope walkers, jugglers, clowns, a lion taming act, trapeze artists, elephants, trick horse riders, acrobats, and magicians. The very last act was someone riding a horse up a ramp and diving into an above-ground swimming pool! Oh, but that was not at all as exciting as the act just before it.

The Arena got pitch black. There were hushed whispers all around and
Then—THEN—IT HAPPENED!!!!!!!!!

POW, POW, POW, POW, POW, POW, POW, POW, POW, POW, POW, POW, POW.

My heart nearly burst to the tune of————

Dum, dum, da-dum, dum,

Da-da-dum, da-dum, dum, dum. . .

And racing out from behind a big black curtain——

There he was——

Riding his horse straight across the Arena right toward us!

I could not believe my eyes!!!!

I screamed, I cried, I smiled so big that my face ached!!!!

THE RIFLEMAN!!!!
THE RIFLEMAN!!!!
THE RIFLEMAN!!!!

I had watched every episode of *The Rifleman* that I could without fail, and there he was right before my eyes! Even now, my heart skips a beat thinking about it. He rode around the ring several times, and I have no clue what he did after that! I was in total shock! Outside of Dad, the Rifleman was my greatest hero, and he was right there! Right in front of me! I could not do anything at all! That was the absolutely most exciting thing that had ever happened to me to that point!

18 – Perfect Attendance

*N*ine days after the excitement of seeing the Rifleman, Chuck Connors, another development came on the horizon. It was toward the end of my kindergarten school year. Up to then, I had perfect attendance. That was evidently some great achievement to Mrs. Ameiss, my teacher. She encouraged us to be there every day so we could receive an award at the end of the year.

Well, you can imagine the dilemma when the ensuing commotion erupted. On a Friday morning in May, about the time when I was to go to school, Dad and Mom started racing around the house like mice being chased by cats. Terri and I had no clue as to what the ruckus was all about. Mom started tensely shouting out things like, "Get Floyd and get Dorothy!" The next thing we knew, we were in the back yard as Floyd and Dorothy were given instructions concerning us. Before we could get any sense to the matter, Dad and Mom raced out to the car and left us standing there. I do not think they even kissed us goodbye!

Remember, Floyd was the mechanic who rented the carriage house for a car repair shop. There was an alley next to the shop that separated our property from the house next door. That is where Dorothy and her husband and their many children lived (probably eight at that time).

I took one look at Floyd and Dorothy, and sheer panic sunk in! It was a school day, and apparently, Dad and Mom had totally forgotten about it, and on top of this, I had already missed the school bus! Knowing that Floyd had a car, I looked up at his face and pleaded with him to take me to school. He looked down at my pitiful panic and very apprehensively asked, "Do you know where your school is?"

I appealed, "No, but I can point!"

Thinking of another way he could discourage the perfect solution, he inquired, "Do you know your left from your right?" I had not been exposed to that information, so I could not convince him that the trip would be a successful adventure. Being afraid of a wild goose chase and not knowing how long our parents would be gone, he simply told me that he did not think that he could take me to school. I was so terribly disappointed!

Dorothy gathered up a few things and escorted Terri and me to her house. We were glad to be with her and her children, especially Margaret, Judy, and Mary. We played all day over there, not knowing where Dad and Mom had gone. We must have stayed with them for a few days.

It was not long before we found out the reason for all that had happened. Dad brought Mom home from the hospital, carrying our brand new baby sister! We were told that her name was Kimberly. Mom had given her that name because the sparkles in the ceiling of the delivery room reminded her of the diamond mine in the Kimberley region in South Africa. (Consistent with her name, Kim has always had an intense fascination with diamonds.)

Kim was a real cutie! She was so tiny and had the prettiest curly dark brown hair and big blue eyes. Terri and I had blue eyes and were both born with black hair, which fell out and turned blonde. Dad always kidded and tried to convince me that his hair fell out when I got mine! Mom wanted a dark-haired, brown-eyed child to take after her. She prayed that Kim would keep the dark hair and that her eyes would turn brown. The brown eyes were not to be.

It probably seems very strange that Terri and I did not realize that Mom was having a baby. I know that we would have been thrilled at the thought. However, Mom had lost our two little brothers before they were born, and her mother had lost three babies. She was probably afraid to tell us.

Once we found out that we had our little sister, the frustration of having missed school turned into elation. We began to turn our hearts to the new addition. Now it made sense why Dad and Mom moved into another room as they began to rearrange the front bedroom for three girls!

To celebrate the new arrival, Dad and Mom invited some of our family members during the Fourth of July weekend. Grandma was always smiling around us. Aunt Doris would rather tease anyone around her than eat ice cream on a blistering hot day. Uncle Porter was blond and very good looking. The three of them drove in from Arkansas. Aunt Anna, Mom's sister, flew in from Pennsylvania. She was short in stature, long in laughter, and very pretty. She had beautiful dark brown hair like our Mom and was very friendly.

Dad, wanting to film the gathering, called us all out to the front yard. Terri and I waved our American flags. I wore my recently acquired white graduation cap with all the pride and dignity of a wise and knowledgeable pre-first-grader. Grandma proudly carried her new grand-baby through the yard as others mingled around her. Aunt Doris, ran around giggling and hugging necks and snapped pictures with her Brownie camera. Dad captured shots of each family member, both singly and in groups. After celebrating on Sunday, the Arkansas family members headed back home, but Aunt Anna was able to stay for another week for Kim's Christening on the 12th of July.

Aunt Anna was Kim's Godmother, and Peanuts from upstairs was chosen to be her Godfather. (Godparents acted as witnesses for the Christening of babies in the Lutheran and other churches. They were asked to keep their Godchildren in prayer during their lives.) Kim was Christened in Grace Lutheran Church. The ceremony was beautiful! The celebration at home lasted all day.

On a side note, poor Aunt Anna became the target of Dad's teasing when she stayed too long in the bathroom. When he could wait no longer, in great laughter, he called out to her, "Shoot Luke or drop the gun!" Of course, that produced rounds of laughter and good-natured teasing for the rest of the evening. It was not long, and she also headed home.

Later that year, Aunt Anna gave three beautiful dolls to us. They were dressed up with bridal gowns and veils, pearl necklaces, high-heeled shoes, and a bouquet and were about eighteen inches tall. I always thought it was kind of funny that she gave a blonde doll to Kim and brunette dolls to Terri and me as that was directly opposite our hair colors! To this day, I still have my brunette doll, though it is a little worn after so many years.

19 – Water, Water, Everywhere

$\mathcal{W}$e vacationed every other year in the northeastern United States. The trek took us from St. Louis and through the states of Illinois, Indiana, Michigan, Ohio, Pennsylvania, New York, New Jersey, Maryland, Virginia, West Virginia, Kentucky, and back home.

During the summer of 1959, the five of us cozily piled into the big seats of the Belair and aimed toward Greenfield Village in Dearborn, Michigan. The first leg of the trip led us to Henry Ford's museum, also known as the Edison Institute. The stately red brick building housed a tremendous amount of technological inventions spread out on rows upon rows of tables in massive rooms. The surrounding factory windows lit the feast for any engineer's eyes aided by the industrial lighting hanging from the ceilings. We were still a little young to appreciate all that held the utmost attention of Dad, and he tried to point out things that would interest us as much as possible.

I think his most favorite thing to do was not so much seeing the sites but the reactions of his daughters to each new experience, and he prolifically set the encounters to come. This would be his attitude toward all the adventures he orchestrated for us throughout his life. (Looking back on the joy on his face in his later years while discussing future intended expeditions with grown family members and distant generations touches my heart. What might have been was abruptly cut short when he left this world at the age of sixty-eight.)

The next morning, we left Detroit, Michigan, and traveled into Ontario, Canada. Following Kings Highway 3, along the northern perimeter of massive Lake Erie heading east, we encountered the largest body of water we girls had seen. As we traveled the beautifully tree-lined route, Dad pointed out ships as we passed. He also related his observations of the models and designs of the automobiles in Canada, drawing attention to the differences between them and the corresponding American cousins.

About five or six hours later, we were standing at the incredible Niagara Falls! Dad wrangled the movie camera while escorting his girls to the railing to get a better view of the water surging toward the roar of the falls. We lingered for just a short while as Dad wanted to grab a bite to eat and check into our hotel. His bigger plan brought us back after dark to observe the falls lit at night in all their glory! The feast of alternating colors illuminating the cascading white waters gave the illusion of a gigantic rush of fruit-flavored crushed ice for snow cones pouring into the lower basin.

We returned the next day to learn more, and to observe the enormous volume and deafening acoustics of the falls. It was amazing to view the powerful force water had carving the cliffs over which it hurled. Niagara Falls is the second largest falls in the world and is one of North America's seven natural wonders. They are fed by the Niagara River flowing down from Lake Erie, which divides at Goat Island, comprising three falls. The Horseshoe Falls, being the most magnificent, flow from the Canadian and United States borders while the American Falls and the Bridal Veil Falls border the United States. Niagara is a native American word meaning thundering water and that they are! Driving around on the Canadian side of the falls, we were impressed by the numerous gardens full of brightly colored flowers and the more formal appearance of the landscape.

Morning light found us on the road again, making our way to Trumansburg, New York, northwest of Ithaca, and situated between the two largest of the Finger Lakes: Seneca and Cayuga. What a charming area for Dad's sister, our Aunt Kay, Uncle Cal, and their family to live. Our cousins, Patty and Barbara, were much older than we were but fun to be around. They had very different personalities. Patty was the oldest and a blonde. I usually shadowed her as much as possible. Terri loved being around Barbara, who had dark red hair and a great personality. Cousin Jimmy was six months older than me and was all boy, complete with a great desire to dissect frogs with broken pieces of glass! Yuck!

Our trips to Aunt Kay's were never complete without a family picnic at one of the lakes. On one occasion, Dad and Mom determined that it would be great fun to take us swimming. I never swam in a lake and was not particularly trustful about getting into the dark water. Dad held me and went out to about four feet deep. Then he and Mom thought playing catch with me would be delightful. So, already terrified, I was tossed by Dad to Mom, and then Mom tossed me back. This happened for a few rounds, and then, oops, somebody did not catch me! Down I went into the murky water. In a panic, I looked around, and all I could see was some dim sunlight filtering through the green water. I could not see either of my parents! Finally, someone reached into my green abyss and pulled me into the air. I screamed, and they tried to calm me down, but somehow, I sensed an air of amusement from them. As soon as I could get my feet on the ground, there was no way they were going to get me back to the water! I did gain a very healthy respect for lakes and dark waters from the ordeal.

A few days passed, and we were on the road again, heading for Hazleton, Pennsylvania. At the time, I had no idea the area held so much of Mom's family history. It was not until I was in my fifties that layers upon layers of family tragedies unfolded in my genealogical research. Both of Mom's parents were born in Hazleton and were each bereft of a parent as toddlers. Grandma's mother and Granddad's father and grandfather all died within a two-year period in the early 1900s. Hardship abounded in their early years. Sadly, they had that in common. They married in Philadelphia, where they raised their family.

Grandma passed away after the birth of their twelfth child. Granddad did the best he could to keep the family together, but after a year, the nine surviving children were split up. The boys, Bud and Dietz, went to Amish farms. The girls, Emily, Kass, and Doris, were sent to a Lutheran children's home. Jackie was adopted by friends in New Jersey. Anna, who had polio as a little girl, needed special care, so Grandma's younger brother, Harry, and his wife, Millie, took her to live with them in Hazleton. Mom, being the oldest and twelve at the time, spent a year with her grandmother and then with other relatives until she was old enough to be on her own. The baby, Porky, was kept by Grandma's best friend during the day. She had thirteen older children of her own. She became a widow, and seven years later, Granddad married her.

In Hazleton, we visited with Great Uncle Harry, Great Aunt Millie, and Aunt Anna, who was still living with them. Great Uncle Harry was short and stout, and Great Aunt Millie was tall, and both were so happy to see us.

The next day we started visiting Mom's family and friends in Philadelphia. The most important family visit was to see Granddad. He was tall like Dad, but dark-haired with an olive complexion. He was rather quiet and did not seem to know what to say to us. I met Grandma Mary, his second wife, who had short white hair but was long on smiles and had sparkling eyes. Our visit with them was very sweet but all too fleeting.

A short day trip led us to Atlantic City, New Jersey, for a stroll on the boardwalk and a chance to see the Atlantic Ocean. It was vast like Lake Erie and bigger than the noisy Niagara Falls yet filled with powerfully relentless and rambunctious waves that could not make up their minds if they were coming or going. This vacation certainly was an excellent primer for the study of the different bodies of water.

20 – Zealous to Serve

By first grade, my lack of self-confidence received a little reprieve. Miss Palmquist was my teacher, and she was every child's dream of kindness and acceptance. Her classroom was bright, cheerful, and as welcoming as she was.

I struggled with reading, but I really loved how she taught us using the big flashcards with the words on them. Observing my challenges, she placed me in a group for children who needed a little more encouragement. It was much to the dismay of Mom and Dad, who thought I did not need the help. Even though my parents read a lot themselves, they never took the time to read to us.

While I had some trouble reading, I evidently had no trouble winning the heart of a certain young red-headed boy who rode on the same bus that I did. He decided to convey his interest by giving me his new school picture one afternoon on the way home. When I walked into our house carrying a picture of a boy, Mom was totally surprised. The photograph package from the school provided only one eight by ten picture, which obviously was for the parents. The boy mistakenly thought that he should be able to give it away, and therefore I was his choice as the recipient. Mom set me straight and called the boy's mother. She reassured her that I would return the picture. They agreed we were both far too young to start a relationship, although they both thought the idea was kind of cute.

On the other hand, when Dad heard the story, he realized that his protective father genes probably needed to start kicking in. I do not remember seeing the boy on the bus after that. I was probably much more interested in playing the clapping games and singing songs with the girls anyway.

Once a week, Miss Palmquist had an activity called "show and tell." I did not have anything to share one day, and when it was my turn, I nervously said so. I thought that I was going to be in trouble. To my amazement, she did not miss a beat. With the warmest and most understanding smile, she said, "Jilene, will you please sing a song for us?" Cold fear melted from my heart. It was replaced with the warmest feeling of encouragement! I stepped forward to the front of the room and broke out into "Twinkle, Twinkle Little Star!" At first, I was quiet and timid, but with each phrase, more confidence welled up until the end when I felt like the most loved person in the world. Ah, Miss Palmquist! I loved her so much!

On another show-and-tell day, I was able to bring in something Dad brought back from one of his travels. He stopped by a cotton farm and obtained a ripened cotton plant that had been "chopped." Dad pulled apart one of the cotton balls and revealed the seeds to us. I was very anxious to share it with the class, as most of us were not familiar with farming.

During that year, I became very perceptive of the order of things in the classroom. We had our Bible time, reading, and math in the morning. Then we had lunch, followed by handwriting, grammar, art, music, snack time, social studies, and science.

One afternoon, as Miss Palmquist led the class to the playground, I stayed behind, hoping to surprise her by doing something that always seemed to please her. One of the chores that was done at the end of every day was cleaning the blackboards. I was so excited! As soon as everyone was gone, I gleefully grabbed the chalk eraser and dutifully cleaned each and every board, all the while imagining her sparkling eyes and a smile across her lovely face when she saw the clean blackboards. As soon as I finished, I hurried to my seat in great expectation of the look of joy on her face as she received her surprise! Moments later, the door opened, and the members of my class scurried to their seats for the afternoon lessons. Then, Miss Palmquist entered the room, and with an astonished look on her face, she, with a well-guarded crushed heart, inquired as to who had erased the boards. My well-meant but naive little gift of surprise rendered my teacher anything but happiness and gratitude as she made it very clear to me that what I had done was erase the entire afternoon's lessons. I was not only in trouble, but I was devastated to think that I had hurt her. She remained kind to me despite this incidence. She showed me that a good teacher is more interested in the outcome of her student than the setbacks along the way. Her caring nature was so encouraging to me.

For Mother's Day, Miss Palmquist had a really nice craft she led us to do. We collected clean eggshells and baby food jars and brought them to class. She spread newspaper out and told us to take the jars and roll them across the eggshells until they were completely crushed into tiny pieces. She had us "paint" the sides of the jars with a generous amount of glue. Then we rolled the wet jars over the crushed eggshells until no glue could be seen. The jars were set aside to dry overnight, and the next day we painted them with gold paint. I could not wait to take my gift home to Mom when the time came. She kept her "trinket" jar for a long time, and each time I saw it, I was reminded of the excitement of making and giving a gift to someone I loved. It is a beautiful blessing to teach someone how to make something, encouraging their good work, and teaching them how to give from the heart.

Miss Palmquist was one of the most influential people in my life. We finished first grade, and she left at the end of the school year. I never saw her again after that but have thought of her so many times over the years. I even searched for her on the internet without any success. I always wanted to tell her how much she meant to me!

21 - The Picnic That Was Not

Our biggest activity of the summer was softball. Dad played on the men's church team. We loved going to the games, not because we were interested in them, but because it was a great opportunity to meet other families and play with the other children. The games were held in the ball fields across the street from Grace Lutheran Church and between Pagedale Police Department and Concord Lutheran School on Ferguson Avenue. That gave us access to all the playground equipment and put us close enough for the Moms to keep one eye on the little ones and the other on their husbands' game.

During one of the games, Terri was running in the area outside the boundary of left field when a fly ball was fouled, and she got clobbered right on the forehead! She wound up with a big goose egg! Bless her heart! From then on, we were pretty much relegated to the playground.

After the games, we met with the other players' families at a local pizza restaurant. They had an outdoor seating area, which made for a warm and friendly gathering. What I remember the most were the strings of red, white, and green lights and red and white checkered tablecloths. Delicious pizza, big pitchers of soda for the kids, and iced tea and beer for the adults filled the tables. Best of all, we enjoyed all the laughter and running around with the other kids!

One Saturday, the men's softball team from the church held a picnic at an out-of-town location. To get to the park, we got up before dawn, packed all the supplies, including a playpen for Kim. We were on the highway just as the sun was coming up.

We made the usual pit stop about halfway to our destination. The gas station attendant filled the tank with gas, while we went in to use the facilities. As we returned to the lobby, Dad handed Kim over to Mom, and the two of them headed out to the car. He then escorted Terri and me to the vending machines we spotted on the way in. Since we left so early, we did not have breakfast. The candy machine became our go-to. Terri and I stood before the glass deliberating over the selections. We got to insert the coins for the purchases, which, for little girls, was always a delight because it made us feel big. Terri pulled the knob, which released a candy bar with chocolate and rice, and I pulled the knob connected to the candy bar with chocolate and peanuts. We quickly consumed our breakfast treat and climbed into the backseat of the car.

It was turning out to be a gorgeous day. The wind was blowing through the open windows whipping wisps of hair across our faces. The sky was a crystal blue, and the sunlight filtered through the beautiful leaves on the trees along the sides of the road, causing shadows to dance across our laps. We were very excited to get to the park and play with our friends.

In an hour or so later, we coasted through the main entrance of the park. We were all gawking out the windows looking for the signs leading to our designated picnic area. "Hurry, hurry, Daddy! There are our friends!" we cried as Dad pulled across to the unpaved parking area set up so that everyone could be close to their supplies.

We anxiously unloaded the car. Mom and Dad set up the playpen by a table near a tree, and Mom spread out a blanket. They busily chatted with friends. The men grabbed their ball equipment to gather for a game of softball before lunch. The women tried to keep watchful eyes on their children while discussing the foods each one brought.

We were released to play with our friends and tore across the field to catch up with them when all of a sudden, I began to feel terrible! I turned to go back to Mom, holding my stomach and head! A rush of heat hit me, and I felt so weak. Once I got to Mom, she took one look at me and felt my forehead. I was burning up, and my skin was turning bright red and itching like fire as a huge rash quickly spread over my skin. Mom, in controlled panic, called for someone to go and get Dad. No one seemed to know what was happening to me. In just a few minutes, Dad was there looking me over with great concern. He told Mom to stay at the picnic with my sisters, and they agreed that it was best for him to take me and get to a hospital as fast as he could. Grabbing me up into his arms, he swept me away to the car.

Apparently, we were more than two hours away from the hospital, and being that it was a weekend, we could not go to see a local doctor. Dad embraced his ability to get to his destinations quickly. We barreled along the highway, reaching the maximum speed he could safely use. I was in the back, and each time we climbed a hill, my small frame lifted slightly from the seat as the car switched from ascent to descent.

I called to Dad, "Why are you driving so fast?" To tell you the truth, we were both pretty scared, and his actions made me a little nervous!

He replied, "Where is the sheriff when you need one?"

He drove in this relentless pace reaching St. Louis and barely slowed to exit the highway. He hoped to draw the attention of the long arm of the law to get an escort to the hospital. Finally, his deliberate lawlessness was rewarded with a flashing red light, and a siren just blocks before reaching the hospital. Dad quickly pulled over, and as calmly as he could muster, he moved to approach the officer. The look on his face explained everything, as the words flew out of his mouth, "I have to get my daughter to the hospital! She is very sick!!!"

Hastily, the officer jumped back into his car and pulled out in front of Dad with red light flashing and siren blaring as he escorted us to the hospital emergency entrance. As Dad parked the car and gathered me into his arms, the officer hopped out of his car and led us into the waiting area. Then he tried to expedite the situation by drawing the nurse's attention to get help for us.

My poor dad was frantic! Of course, the nurse tried to assure him that they would help and started asking questions to fill out the paperwork. He shot out the answers as quickly as possible to hurry the process along. She asked how old I was, and he instantly replied, "Six!"

I looked up at him and said, "No, Daddy, I'm seven!" It did not matter to him how old I was as he just wanted immediate attention for me.

As the nurse was completing the questionnaire, she led us into an examining room and directed a doctor toward us. In a very short time, the doctor checked me out. Finally, he asked what I had eaten. With that identification being made, he determined that I must have had an allergic reaction to the candy bar, which presented itself as hives. That was really strange as Dad told the doctor that I had no problem with chocolate or peanuts before. Apparently, some allergies come and go. I have never had that reaction from chocolate or peanuts again.

By this time, I was starting to feel a little better. We left the emergency room armed with a prescription and instructions for using calamine lotion. We headed for the car, and I slept all the way back to the park. Dad was feeling better also. We got to the picnic about the time everyone was packing up to leave. We followed suit, and as the sun was setting, we rolled into our driveway at home.

Slathering calamine lotion all over my hives became the evening's entertainment as we settled in exhausted from the day's ordeal.

22 - Where Dreams Were Made

The girls' bedroom in the front of the house was a very special place to me. My bed was tucked under the window on the east side of the house with an early morning view of the sun rising above the used car lot across the street.

Across from my bed was Mom's telephone bench, one of her most cherished possessions. It was fashioned out of cherrywood in very graceful lines. Scrollwork adorned its back, and the seat was upholstered in an antique red brocade. A ledge for the black rotary dialed phone was on the right side. Tucked underneath was a shelf for the massive St. Louis telephone directories. The hardback binders they were bound in were at least four inches thick as the St. Louis area neared one and a half million residents. The directories were updated every year. There was enough room under the shelf to stash additional books and literature. A black-and-white family photo of me standing beside the telephone bench in nothing but a diaper and a great big smile was snapped in 1954.

Mom spent quite a lot of time on the phone, and she had an interesting doodling habit she developed in the duration. Papers upon papers were filled with her circle pencil art, and all of them complete with shading. She particularly liked drawing grapes and swirls. This was a past time for her while she made calls for school, Girl Scouts, softball, ladies aid, church, or any other activity we were involved in. Her lists were laid out in order on the makeshift desk, which was my bed.

For younger readers, making phone calls in the 1950s and 1960s would be considered a grand production compared to the twenty-first century. First of all, telephone portability was limited to the length of the electric cord by which they were connected to the nearest wall. In my early youth, I remember Mom and Dad complaining about the party line system used before private phone lines were available. No, that had nothing to do with political party lines. It meant that several neighbors' phones were wired through to the same outside telephone lines. When any one of them on the party line used their phones, no one else could make a call. Phone etiquette was not always employed, and on occasion, things could get a little tense. By the late 50s, we were the proud owners of a private line! Local calls were self dialed. Long-distance calls required the use of a telephone operator to "put through" the connection after dialing the number O. Choices could be made at that point as to whether the caller or receiver would be responsible for the call's payment. Today, dialing a number is touch or even voice-activated. Though tempted, I will not articulate the historical instructions for activating phones from that time period even though many might find it fascinating. Suffice it to say, it was a much longer process requiring precision, patience, and sometimes a sore index finger.

On another note, a ringing phone was like an alarm to cease activity to answer the beckoning sound. If Dad was not at home, the thunder of little feet was heard as a race ensued to answer first with the prize being a little personal conversation with him.

Beyond the telephone or "gossip" bench were the free-standing metal clothes cabinets and sufficient ironing space. Terri and Kim's trundle beds that Dad constructed lay in front of the blocked french doors to the hallway.

Next to their beds and below the front windows, a fancy radiator painted an antique gold color sat on the wooden floor. It had a matching flat metal cover that became our window seat to the world outside when not used for heat. At any time, one of us could be found perched there as if it were a vehicle taking us on journeys of our imagination. It was a place of comfort and quiet for contemplating deep thoughts or just enjoying the beauty of God's creation.

Open windows during pleasant weather allowed a refreshing draft through the room. It smelled so clean after a rain shower or when the grass was cut. Sometimes, I would just lay down on the radiator, peer out at the big beautiful cumulus clouds in the bright blue summer sky and watch airplanes come through what looked like enormous clusters of cotton balls. When Dad flew to his work destinations, I would wonder if any of those planes were bringing him home to us. It was hard to understand why he traveled so much.

There I contemplated the wisdom of Solomon in his early life and prayed for that kind of wisdom. I also prayed that when I grew up and had grandchildren, we would spend a lot of time together. That was such a deeply rooted memory to me, for I longed to have time with my only grandmother in Arkansas and my only grandfather in Pennsylvania. We usually took three short trips to see Grandma each year, but there was never any one-on-one time involved in the visits. I only remember seeing Granddad once or twice and then for only an hour or two. *The New Basic Readers*, featuring Sally, Dick, and Jane, exposed me to the concept of having a personal relationship with grandparents. The picture of their grandmother serving them freshly baked cookies still warm on the cookie sheet convinced me it was so. Missing a relationship with grandparents left an overwhelming vacuum in my young life that yearned for fulfillment.

During fair weather evenings, we could hear the sounds of diminishing traffic as the sun was setting. From the direction of downtown St. Louis, we could hear the rumbling of heavy wooden carts with metal wheels as they were pushed along the curbs of Page Boulevard. The voices of three or four ambitious twelve-to-fourteen-year-old newspaper boys filled the air with loud cries of, "Post Dispatch" and "St. Louis Globe!" Customers who wanted the daily newspapers hastily made their way from the homes and businesses to these vendors. The daily news was purchased for ten cents, but Sunday papers fetched twenty-five cents and were only sold on Saturday nights. All stores were closed on Sunday in St. Louis.

An elderly lady who rented the front apartment upstairs often asked Terri or me to get the paper for her from the boys. She tried to pay us for our effort, but Mom wanted us to learn to serve others, so we were told to kindly decline the offer. She was very grateful to us, though.

We so enjoyed the many things we viewed from our "window seat." Spring and fall brought colorful displays to the world. Of course, winter snows were especially interesting when the snowflakes flew near and landed on the windows. We could see each delicate flake's beautiful uniqueness before it melted on the glass or combined with others to form piles on the window ledges, porch railings, sidewalks, and yard. At Christmas, Dad decorated the window frames with colored lights, which made watching the evening snowfalls more exciting. Being on a busy street, we often saw cars sliding from one place to another as they lost traction on the slippery slush on the road, all the while hoping no one would be hurt. These were the outside views we explored.

On the playful note, the radiator cover became a stage for our dolls. The two I remember the most were named Philene and Star Heaven. I know Star Heaven was a little unusual, but I enjoyed looking at the stars at night, and she reminded me of them with her dark hair and bright eyes. I made up the name Philene because it rhymed with my name, and Mom told me that Philadelphia was the "City of Brotherly Love." So I took "Phil" and "ene" and put them together. These dolls were similar to the new Barbie™ dolls, and they could wear Barbie™ style clothes.

In the other corner, by the radiator, was a large pink-and-blue toy chest that we thoroughly enjoyed. It was almost as tall as we were and had two doors with removable chalkboards on the top half. Behind the doors were two shelves. Terri and I split the top half between us. The bottom half housed our larger toys, including red plastic bricks similar to legos for making houses, tinker toys, and skate cases. I had such a great time keeping all my books and school supplies organized on the top shelf and my doll case with all the clothes on the bottom shelf. My first book that Mom and Dad gave to me was *A Child's Garden of Bible Stories*. The inscription says that they gave it to me in 1959. My other favorite books were my *Holy Bible, The Lutheran Hymnal, Little Visits With God, More Little Visits with God, Growing in Christ*, and two Lutheran Prayer Books, a book about Helen Keller, and *The Diary of Anne Frank*. It also housed books that were purchased from the school book fairs like *Lilies of the Field*. The shelf became temporary storage for library books, especially *Heidi* and *Charlotte's Web*. We had jewelry boxes that held our necklaces, pins, and rings. They were enlisted to provide double duty as "cash registers" when we played store or restaurant. The chalkboards became signs to promote our various "sales" or "menu items" as the case arose.

Between the toy box and my bed, the blond-colored nine-drawer dresser stood in front of the walled-up fireplace. I loved the simplicity of the construction. Each daughter was issued three drawers. The top displayed wooden crosses we made in Girl Scouts, jewelry boxes, softball trophies, and other trinkets we had collected over the years.

We each had green and white wool blankets printed with maple leaves in the design on our beds. The bedspreads were made of light purple chenille about the color of clover. They were fuzzy and fun to rub your fingers across to trace the rows of designs in the textures. Above my head hung a picture of Jesus standing at the door knocking. It represented the Bible verse, "Behold, I stand at the door and knock. If anyone hears My voice and opens the door, I will come in and dine with him and he with Me." Revelation 3:20, KJV[c]. The door in the picture has no handle on the outside. It portrays that the only way Jesus comes in is if someone opens the door to Him. I opened that door when I was little, which has made all the difference in the world to me! I am so glad that the picture was in our bedroom so I could see it every day. It is the first thing you see today when entering my home to remind all who enter of His faithful love.

23 – Peanut Butter Balls and Scary Basements

Dad was handy both inside and outside the house. He had not only replaced the porch out front, but also the porch and staircase from the master bedroom to the backyard. It led to a narrow sidewalk on the street side of the house. He replaced the original white picket fence that marked the yard's boundary with a six-feet-tall redwood fence for more privacy. A big wooden ranch-style gate extended from the fence to the mechanics' garage. Two silver maple trees stood inside the fence and, like the red maple out front, acted like soldiers guarding our yard. A shorter redwood fence separated the yard into two sections: one for the play and laundry areas and the other for the burn barrels and a place to park. We did not have trash pick-up, so we burned our garbage and trash out there. A giant red oak tree with its large leaves stood providing ample shade in the southwest corner of the outer yard. The backyard was a place of dreams and imagination! The surrounding tree canopy left a wide-open patch of sunlight, affording a beautiful place for my sisters and me to play out the things that crossed our minds.

A swing set with the double-seater swing, three single swings, and a slide took center stage in the yard. When Kim was old enough, Dad made a baby swing for her out of wood. In the rare moments that I was alone in the backyard, I would get on the swing and go as high as possible. Then I thought that my only audience was God. I made up little songs and sang them just for Him. I looked up at the clouds or the clear blue sky with each upward swing and hoped that He would reach down and touch me. I wanted to be in His company, and I now can look back and feel the warmth of His pleasure in my little gifts and faith.

The sidewalk between the play area and the laundry area was the highway for our little yellow metal pedal convertible sports car. It extended to the other part of the yard, so we felt like we were taking big trips from our "garage" under the staircase to the outer yard and back. That lasted until we were too big to fit into our car.

In the summer, Dad set up a rectangular-shaped kiddie swimming pool between our racing sidewalk and the laundry lines and poles. Mom set Kim in her cloth diaper to play in the water. She did a poopie. I did not realize it. Since I finished first grade, I was familiar with peanut butter balls from the school lunches. I reached into the water and said, "Mommy, look at the peanut butter balls!!!" She grabbed me and kept me from making a huge mistake as she informed me what they really were. It was a challenge to face peanut butter balls after that!

Mom used to let us pretend we were making homemade pies using leftover frozen pot pie aluminum tins after rainstorms. Mud, pebbles, weeds, and grass were the basic ingredients for every pie we could imagine. One day, I tried to bend one of the tins and accidentally sliced my hand with it. Bloody, muddy pies resulted in our resident health inspector (Mom) shutting down our bakery. Culinary experiences were relegated to future years.

Terri and I both had birthday parties in the backyard. I think I was seven when I had mine. The yard was filled with children from my class, and we played pin the tail on the donkey. Dad got plastic banana split boats from the Dairy Queen®, and we tried to throw pennies into them. Everyone got to keep all the pennies that stayed in the boats. Dad did hat tricks for us, and then we went in for cake and ice cream and opening presents. My favorite gift was a stuffed Scottie Dog. I put a "leash" on it and drug it all over the house until Mom got tired of it and threw it in the burn barrel. My heart was broken.

We did have a real dog, but only for a few weeks. We named it Trixie after the cereal Trix®. Mom did not like the real dog either and got rid of it while we were not home.

Next to the clothesline area was a beautiful white snowball bush and a purple hibiscus bush. Occasionally, Mom stood beside them at the fence to talk with the next-door neighbors. Two magnificent black walnut trees from their yard shaded that corner of our yard.

Most mothers were very protective of their floors when they were washing them. Mom followed suit and forbade us to be underfoot while she was in the process or walk on them while they were drying. Her method of safeguarding the wet floors was relegating us to the backyard. She then prevented our re-entry by locking the back door with the chain lock.

To many, that would seem a demise of little consequence. For little girls who need to use the facilities, this action could provide serious anguish. Her alternative plan was for us to use the bathroom in the dreaded basement! No! Not the basement! Yes, the basement! It was the creepiest place on earth to me when I was a child.

The bathroom in the basement could only be reached by going down the concrete steps that led to an old wooden swinging door. Behind that creaking door were two four-feet-high concrete walls flanking a six-feet-long walkway to a green wooden basement door with the dusty glass window. Those walls held back the dirt underneath the house. There was about a three-feet-high crawl space that gave access to pipes under the first floor. It was dark, dank, and foreboding.

If that was not bad enough, you only had seconds to make it through the basement door before you heard the rusty spring slam the swinging door behind, leaving you in sheer and utter darkness! Once actually inside the basement, racing another ten feet, the chain pull from the hanging ceiling light could be reached. The walls in the basement were all unpainted concrete and dark with age. Two small, dusty spider-web-covered windows on the basement's street side revealed the dirt floor of the long-neglected coal storage area of decades past.

If weather had been inclement, sheets hung on lines in the basement, perhaps hiding monsters or other creatures. The great big boiler was in the opposite corner standing, like a giant metal robot that gurgled sounds of water being heated for steam. The other corner housed a double-doored closet deep enough to lay shovels and rakes and other long tools, but my imagination insisted that it had once been the resting place for the caskets of mummies. An unpainted wooden staircase led back upstairs to a door that remained locked. All was relatively dark down there.

Now the worst part of all was . . . the bathroom! Just another ten feet from that hanging light, a threateningly dark stall stood without a door. A lone, aged, stained toilet with a black seat sat in the middle of the unlit partitioned off room, perhaps hiding someone's pet alligator that had been flushed somewhere else in the city. It just might resurface from the sewer system just as I was in that vulnerable position. My heart pounded in my throat every time I had to go there. I was totally terrified!

After a while, I could no longer take the chilling dangers of accessing the basement bathroom. A brilliant idea entered my head so that I could be freed from torment! I got a stick from one of the silver maple trees. Slowly, I crept up the staircase to the back door of the first floor of the house. Very quietly and gradually, I twisted the doorknob and pushed the door open to where I could see the chain lock. I took my stick and very patiently but intently and carefully fished for the catch on the last link of the chain lock and slid it to the opening on the track. Quietly pulling the door almost shut, I unseated the sliding piece on the chain to get access to the first floor bathroom.

The only problem was that once I went back outside, I could not re-lock the door. I do not know why, but I did not get into trouble over the incident, and I never used the basement bathroom again!

Many years later, when my sisters and I were grown, married, and with children of our own, we revisited the creepy basement issues with our dad. All of a sudden, compassion welled up, and he told us that had he known that we were all terrified of the basement, he would not have put us through the ordeal. All we could respond with was, "Yeah, right!" as we all rolled our eyes in disbelief!

Note: An excellent point to make here is that chain locks are invariably useless if a child can figure out how to gain entrance despite their use. Another thought, locking children out of the house is not always an effective way to let clean wet floors dry.

Commercial Break

24 - Television

elevision was our primary source of family entertainment. I remember my parent's excitement shopping for our first television set from a furniture store in Wellston, located near the bus station. Dad also bought an antenna (called "rabbit ears") for better reception. He loaded the big wooden box into the trunk of the car and headed home.

There were only four television stations available to us in those years: ABC, NBC, CBS, and a local television station. Color television was not yet developed, so all programming was done in black and white.

Programs began airing around six in the morning with the news. Reruns of older situation comedy programs called "sitcoms" and game shows ran from around nine until noon. That was the time of the beginning of *The Price is Right*, *Let's Make a Deal and Password*. *People are Funny* with *Art Linkletter Show* had skits and a delightful routine of interviewing four young school-age children and awarding them prizes. Mr. Linkletter eventually wrote a funny book called *Kids Say the Darnedest Things*, and they surely do. George Goble and Jack Benny had classic shows also. Comedy was a prominent theme in the 50s.

The news came on at noon and again at six p.m. In between, most homemakers watched "soap operas" full of sappy drama. Mom was included in that group of viewers, and we had better be quiet or make ourselves scarce when those programs were on. Late afternoons were full of kid shows including, *Bozo the Clown, Captain Kangaroo* with Mr. Green Jeans, *Romper Room, Popeye, the Sailor Man, Woody Woodpecker, Rin Tin Tin, Lassie, Mickey Mouse Club, Superman, The Lone Ranger,* and *F Troop* just to name a few. There were other shows that I really did not enjoy because they were so incredibly silly.

Evening and weekend programming was full of comedies, music shows, suspense theaters, westerns, detective shows, doctor shows, spooky mysteries, and space shows. My two sisters and I became very well versed in the cowboy shows, *Rawhide, Maverick, Cheyenne, Wagon Train, Sugarfoot, Have Gun — Will Travel, The Rifleman, Bonanza,* and *Gunsmoke.* Medical shows influenced the apparel industries. *Ben Casey* and *Dr. Kildaire* were so popular that doctor shirts became a standard option for wardrobe even for children to wear to school! The comedies, *Father Knows Best, The Donna Reed Show, The Doris Day Show, The Dinah Shore Show, Make Room for Daddy, Dennis the Menace, Hazel, My Three Sons, Leave It to Beaver, Beverly Hillbillies, The Andy Griffith Show, Mr. Ed, My Favorite Martian,* and *The Dick Van Dyke Show* were big hits with us. *The Man from U.N.C.L.E.* and *The Fugitive* were action-packed. The three shows I enjoyed the most were *The Rifleman, The Loretta Young Show,* and *The Millionaire* as each dealt with character qualities, good values, and sometimes references to God. On Sundays, the four shows I remember watching the most were *Mutual of Omaha's Wild Kingdom, Daniel Boone, Flipper, Shirley Temple Theatre,* and *The Wonderful World of Disney.*

The scary comedies were *The Adam's Family* and *The Munsters,* but the seriously frightening shows were *Twilight Zone, Alfred Hitchcock Presents,* and *The Outer Limits.* They often left me with sleepless hours in the night. It so happened that my parents were out one evening and hired a babysitter for us. We were watching the *Twilight Zone,* and I desperately needed to use the bathroom. All the lights were turned off, and I needed to go through my parents' bedroom. Mom kept the pile of dirty laundry on the floor next to the bathroom. I thought a giant turtle was in the room and was terrified to go in there and begged the babysitter to turn on the light. She would not, and I finally had to face my fear and wade through the dark past the "turtle" and into the bathroom. I wasted no time getting back out of there!

Dad liked to watch wrestling or boxing on the weekends, and never watched football. He did like detective shows like Dragnet, and The Untouchables. He loved to watch *Red Skelton, Car 54 Where Are You?, Candid Camera, and Hee-Haw.*

Mom liked the many music shows that were available. The best singers hosted their own programs, among them being: Nat King Cole, Dean Martin, Andy Williams, Tom Jones, Glen Campbell, Jimmy Dean, Perry Como, Tennessee Ernie Ford, Bing Crosby, and Sonny and Cher. Other musical-themed shows included *Lawrence Welk, Sing Along with Mitch,* and *Name that Tune,* the last two being game shows. Mom and we girls thoroughly enjoyed trying to outguess the contestants.

Our parents enjoyed *The Ed Sullivan Show, The Jack Benny Show, The Bob Hope Show,* and *ALCOA Theatre.* Mom was especially interested in the king of the teen music shows, *American Bandstand* with Dick Clark as it was televised from her hometown, Philadelphia. After it's first fourteen years, the show moved to Los Angeles. Each of these shows was fantastic in its own way, providing listening enjoyment from the venues of classic, contemporary, country music, and much more.

Sometimes Dad came home after a long day to find all of us so engrossed in the final minutes of some television show to the point that we did not realize he had come in. He then made his presence known by saying, "You know they are all gonna die anyway!" That got our attention! Many good endings were missed because of his comment and the agonizing responses to his joke. He got a great big kick out of that, though!

On another note (pun intended), it is surprising how many theme songs from television programs have lingered in our minds that we have not heard for decades. From the children's programs early in the morning to the late-night talk shows and all the commercials between, just a few notes transport us to the times we sat in our living rooms totally engrossed with what we saw and heard.

During the late 1950s and the early 60s, remote controls were not available. We girls sat on the floor as close as we could to watch tv and reach the channel and volume controls. We often got scolded for sitting too close because "everyone knew that sitting next to the television would ruin our eyesight." Sometimes the reception would go out, and it would be our job to fix it. There seemed to be a certain sweet spot on the side of the tv that rendered a perfect picture once whacked with a hand. Quite unscientific, but it worked. My bed happened to sit behind the stereo wall, making me the closest to the tv. If we were sent to bed, but I was still awake when the reception went out, I was called in to give the appropriate whack to the side of the tv. You would think I would be rewarded for my effectiveness with a later bedtime, but that was not the case. I would return to my covers listening to *The Steve Allen Show* or *Jack Paar's The Tonight Show* until I fell fast asleep or until the broadcasting stopped.

At midnight, a recording of the national anthem played, followed by a sign-off picture. An ear-piercing single high-frequency signal announced the end of programming, and the screen went black until the next morning.

25 - Movie Theaters and Drive-Ins

There were five different movie theaters we had the opportunity to visit as we were growing up. Two of them were in Wellston. One movie I especially enjoyed at the Wellston Theater was *Lilies of the Field* with Sidney Poitier. We saw a few scary movies which I did not like at all. When I was ten, Mom hired Margaret, the girl next door, to take Terri and me to the movies. I am pretty sure her sister, Judy, got to go with us. We were each given seventy-five cents. Fifty cents for admission and twenty-five cents for a treat. I had two favorites: Junior Mints® and popcorn. Junior Mints® nearly always won out. It made for a sweet afternoon away from home.

Sometimes Mom took us on the bus to the Tivoli or Varsity Theaters in University City. We saw *Mary Poppins* with Julie Andrews and Dick Van Dyke, *Shenandoah* with James Stewart, and *How The West Was Won* with a huge cast of actors and actresses.

One evening, Dad treated us to dinner in a grand cafeteria somewhere in downtown St. Louis. The building had a gorgeous staircase and seating on both floors. Afterwards, we went to a very beautiful theater nearby to see the movie, *Flubber,* starring Fred MacMurray.

We went to the drive-in theaters several times. For my younger readers, this was a place with a giant outdoor movie screen. Cars parked on semi-circular hilly rows. The parking spaces were separated by poles wired with clunky looking speakers that patrons hung on their car window. Families tried to get the places nearest the bathrooms and concession stands. Some people brought lawn chairs and sat in front of the cars. At least one of the drive-ins had a playground up front for use before the movies started.

Double features with cartoons in between allowed for bathroom and concession stand breaks. It could be difficult at times to see if you were in the back seat, and many children wound up falling asleep in the cars. For our family, the experience would start out to be fun, but Dad hated to be caught in the after movie traffic, so we never got to see the end of the second feature. As soon as it got to be about the last ten minutes of the movie, Dad returned the speaker to the pole and headed for the unpaved exit with all the other impatient patrons who valued escape over movie conclusions. The exiting cars stirred up the dirt, leaving a massive dust cloud behind them. Naturally, windows were rolled up tight to keep the dust out, which was ever so much "fun" since it was usually pretty warm outside. All the escaping vehicles' passengers craned their necks to catch soundless glimpses of the end of the entertainment as drivers tried to hurriedly make their way out to the highway. For many of the films we saw, the endings still remain a mystery.

26 - Popular Music

The sound of music was a huge theme in my life with the family and individually. Rarely a day passed without its constant companionship.

My earliest recollections include riding in the back seat of the car being part of the captive audience to my parents' renditions of silly songs from their childhood or melodies that were popular when they were young adults. On a trip of any distance, Dad without fail sang two of his favorite songs, "Shoo Fly Pie" and "I Can Tell by Your Toes." The latter would always cause groans from his daughters, who did not think it was a bit funny, but his laughter rang louder than our cries for secession! Mom always chimed in with her two favorites, "Mairzy Doats" (1943), and "The Hut-Sut Song" (1941). In self-defense, my sisters and I cheerfully retaliated with the latest of the silly songs we had learned in Girl Scouts, school, bus rides home, television, and, of course, a variety of early childhood nursery rhymes. That got us through hundreds of miles of long trips through the years!

If that was not enough, musical parody became an art form with my parents. We never quite knew what we were going to be bombarded with when they were in a really cheerful mood. Often the practice filled our home with lots of laughter and from time to time, can still bubble up unexpectedly when I am particularly happy.

When they were first married, Mom bought Dad a guitar. He only brought it out occasionally along with his harmonicas, and on rare occasions, he shared little ditties with us. His enjoyment of country music was resisted because Mom had a decided distaste for anything that sounded "twangy". However, he did share "Howling at the Moon" sung by Hank Williams, Sr. It was a pretty funny song about a lovesick man.

Both of our parents loved the music by George Gershwin. He was incredibly talented and composed "Rhapsody in Blue" and "American in Paris" These compositions are intensely filled with emotion and draw images to your mind of life in the big cities. He wrote classical music with a genuinely moving jazz style that grabbed your mind and heart.

For Valentine's Day, one year, Dad bought Mom a stereo hi-fi record player! It stood tall on its four modern looking tapered legs and was the "blond" color so popular at the time. They cranked up that hi fi and danced together in the living room. They had such fun. Dad picked me up and held me in one arm, and Mom picked Terri up and carried her with one arm. Together all four of us danced the jitterbug! When Dad was at work, sometimes Terri and I danced together by ourselves. Mom took a pretty cute picture of that!

The stereo gave us all years of entertainment, and many trips to record stores filled our home with a library of the music of the 1930s through the early 1960s. Mom especially loved the show tunes, big band, and instrumental albums. She had about 100 single records, mostly popular dance and the romance music of the time.

Music in those days was recorded on black vinyl disks that looked like flat plates. Albums were recordings of several tunes or one or two exceptionally long-playing pieces of music. Therefore, they were called LPs for long-play or 33 1/3s because they were played at 33 1/3 rpm (revolutions per minute). They were 12" in diameter, had a small hole in the center, and held about 40 minutes worth of recorded audio on each side. Singles were commonly called 45s as they were played at 45 rpm. They were 7" in diameter, had a hole in the center about 1 1/2", and held about 4 to 5 minutes of recordings on alternate or "flip" sides. The holes kept records centered on spindles on the turntables as they revolved. Both types of records had music on the front and the back or flip sides. Labels in the center of the records displayed the information of the recording artists, studios, and names of the recordings. The packaging for the records were called jackets for the albums and sleeves for both albums and singles. They also displayed artwork, tune titles, the names of the singers, composers, record producers, and sometimes lyrics. Even today, many of these albums are still collectable, and their jackets are highly prized for the artwork.

The music was recorded on the records with grooves that circled the disks starting on the outer edge and making its way to the center. There was a small unrecorded space between each recording to separate them. A special needle held by a metal arm was placed on the outermost groove on the record. As the record spun on the turntable, the sound traveled by wire to the speakers for amplification. Record collections took up a lot of space, and many people bought special racks to hold them as we also did.

The record store was about two blocks east of our house on Page Boulevard. Mom let Terri and I pick out a record of our very own one time. Terri liked Elvis Presley, but I liked Ricky Nelson. We both got 8" x 10" black and white pictures of our favored singers.

By the time I was in fifth grade, I was exposed to more classical music. I saved my money and purchased "The Nutcracker Suite" and "The 1812 Overture", which totally impressed me. Mom started buying recordings of the brass band, called Tijuana Brass and famous singers like Dean Martin and Andy Williams.

Unexpected Treasures

27 - Pointed Toes or Tennis Shoes

About this time in our lives, Mom's interest was piqued to investigate ballet lessons for her two older daughters. She approached Dad with the idea. His response was less than enthusiastic as he shared his opinions that he did not want his daughters to develop muscular-looking legs. No offense to any ballerinas who perchance read this book. Terri was always much more fluid in movement than I was. I am a little on the flat-footed side, which does not lend easily to hopping around and spinning on pointed toe.

However, Dad did develop what he thought would be a suitable substitution for ballet slippers and tutus. Instead of gliding gracefully over the beautiful wooden floors under the sparkling lights of rehearsal halls, he envisioned us racing rampantly through the baselines of the softball fields, successfully sliding into home plate.

Since it was a total given that Dad would have absolutely nothing to do with the former and was enthusiastic about participating in the latter, softball won. I was then the first in our family enlisted to play on a little girl's softball team.

Mom took care of all the details concerning enrollment into the Khoury League, insurance, and apparel, including bright red shorts, white blouse with the number "4" on the back and the company sponsor's name (Spot Sales), white tennis shoes, and socks.

Dad took on the responsibility of purchasing the equipment. He took great care in selecting what he thought would be the best gloves for his daughters. To him, no glove was of any value until the leather was oiled and best shaped into use for the owners's hand. We were given adult-sized gloves, and they swallowed our little hands like Papa Bear's chair swallowed the little girl in the tale of Goldilocks and the Three Bears. He took each glove and worked the neats-foot oil over every inch of leather as we watched with great interest. The oil turned the gloves into darker shades of brown. Then he let us try them on again and explained in great detail where each finger should be placed. We naturally wanted to put our fingers into the matching fingers of the glove. In his wisdom, Dad had us put our first and middle fingers in the glove's middle finger, allowing the first finger to have a little more protection. The technique also gave us a more secure grip in the glove and making the pocket a little more substantial! We were impressed because he was so enthusiastic about it.

Next, he told us never to leave our gloves lying around the house and never leave them in the dirt! When we were finished using them, we were to place a ball in the pocket and roll the glove closed over the ball. Then we were to put a thick rubber band around it to help keep the proper shape for catching balls.

He had also bought a ball and took Terri and me out to the front yard to teach us to catch and throw. After placing us on the street side of the yard to protect the house windows, it became quickly apparent that our ability to catch was even worse than our ability to throw. Also, he had a much better chance of snagging our wild balls, which could have become torpedoes to oncoming cars flying down the four-lane highway in front of our house!

Terri was not old enough to be on the team that year, but she accompanied Dad and me to several practices. I was introduced to the coach who sent me out into the field with the other girls. He began gently hitting balls to us. We probably had some batting practice. I do not remember being taught anything about how the game was played. All I knew was that Dad was excited, and we were basking in the moment with him.

The evening of my very first game came. Mom laid out my neatly ironed uniform. I quickly dressed and scrambled to the kitchen, where we had our regular pre-game dinner of sandwiches and iced tea. The car was loaded for the family event. Grabbing my new prized possession, my glove, I jumped into the car with the rest of the family. Off we headed to the softball diamond in the far end of the ballpark where Dad also played his games.

The two opposing teams took their places on the benches on opposite sides of the home plate. Each team's families and other spectators lined their lawn chairs and blankets in the safety zones. Girls were yelling and screaming and generally having a terrific time. I am sure that a great majority of us were novices baited for our first adventure into organized sports.

The umpire talked to the coaches, and the teams took their places for the first inning. I did not play right away but sat out for a few innings watching. Then the big moment came! The coach told me to head out to right field. He had to tell me where it was, and I walked out there and turned around, trying to figure out exactly where he wanted me. Dad stood as proud as a peacock. Terri sat near Mom who held Kim watching the whole experience, eager to see what would happen. Dad caught my eye and motioned for me to lean down and place my hands with the glove on my knees and watch the batter. The girls were all chattering, "Hey, batter, batter, batter,

batter!" and I chimed in with the rest, not knowing why. You know it, the first batter hit the ball and everyone started screaming! She started running for first base as the ball flew straight out to right field. I was so excited standing there with my hands on my knees watching the ball come out toward me, and I then watched intently as it rolled past me further out into the field. Wow! That was terrific! I looked over at my Dad with the biggest smile on my face! He yelled out to me, "JILENE, WHY DIDN'T YOU CATCH THAT BALL?!?" in sheer disbelief! I happily yelled back to him, "WHY, DADDY? WAS I SUPPOSED TO?" A compassionate roar of laughter invaded the crowd as Dad turned around, lifting his shoulders and hands and shaking his head, chuckling to the silent words, "Do not despise the day of small beginnings!"

I made it through that first game, which was the beginning of seven enjoyable years of playing softball. Dad made it his ambition to train Terri and me as much as possible when he was in town. He pulled out the gear he had for playing a game called "Indian Ball." It was very similar to softball or baseball, but with only two bases, and the bats and balls were considerably smaller. The softball we used in our league was ten inches in circumference. The Indian ball was about six inches in circumference. The bat was as skinny as a broom handle. He figured that if he could get us to catch, throw, and hit that ball, anything bigger would surely be no problem at all. So that is what we practiced with at home in the front yard for catching and throwing. He took us early or stayed after practices to work with us using the Indian bat. His other technique taught us to catch balls aimed straight at our faces. He took it slowly, and when he could tell that we were comfortable with catching, he increased the speed and the strength with which he threw. It was a great challenge, and we took to it like eating ice cream!

The next year, Dad coached the team, and Terri joined the league on a younger team. Mom became the scorekeeper. Over the years, our parents alternated between working with my team and Terri's team when our ages separated us. We loved everything about it except for the time poor Terri was hit right in the stomach when someone was trying to practice her swing before going up to bat. OUCH! I felt so sorry for Terri, and the other girl was also shocked by the incident. The whole team learned FOSB (fear of swinging bats), and we all stayed very clear from that point on.

About the third year into playing softball, my team won an opportunity to play a game that was an hour's distance away. We passed farm fields where beautifully deep green crops deliciously scented the fresh country air. We manned the ball diamond with just enough summer sunlight to battle an intensely close game through to the sixth inning. I played second base and cheered everyone on like a pro and viciously made my, "Hey, batter, batter, batter," cry with the best of them. The subsequent tie committed the teams to one more round for victory. We held the tie as the other team played. When I came up to bat, we had gained runners on first and second base. The pitch came flying toward me, and I smacked it as hard as I could out to left field! My pounding heart pushed my slightly flat feet as fast as it could, and I rounded second base! Everyone on our side was shouting in congratulatory glee and a groan of defeat from the other side. At the same time, I was ecstatic and ready for the challenge to make it to home! Then, to my utter disbelief, everyone stopped playing and started walking to their dugouts. I was dumbfounded and perplexed! It was like ordering a delicious hot fudge sundae with whipped cream, pecans, and a cherry on top and having someone take it away after taking the intensely delicious first bite!

That was my first real introduction to how an overtime game ended when the last needed run was scored. Ugh! I had no idea that I had made the hit for that winning point and could not understand why everyone just stopped playing! Honestly, I wondered if I had done something wrong. It took me awhile to understand the mechanics of the innings of tied games. I had to accept the rules even though I felt robbed. Call me a little crazy, but I secretly think it would be great for the umpires to let the last player finish the job even if the game was over. I guess teaching players about tied games ahead of time would have helped.

In the scheme of things, Dad's motivation and devotion to training Terri and me in the beloved game of softball rewarded him with not one but two pretty good little ball players. Terri reigned supreme on first base and right field, and my domain rotated between second base, shortstop, and left field. Both of us had batting averages of five-hundred. In the eyes of his daughters and many a team member, our dad batted a thousand as a softball dad, coach, and assistant coach. His scheme to avoid ballet by replacing it with softball and putting his whole heart into it worked out fabulously. In our seven-year careers, we played in a few All-Star tournaments including the Missouri-Illinois Championship Games, and we were on teams both in St. Louis and in later years, Ft. Worth, Texas.

To add a lingering flavor to this story, I was motivated to hit the ball as hard and as far as I could, because I hated running. Secondly, Terri and I got to play burnout (who can throw the ball the hardest until the other person gives up) with our Uncle Porter and Cousin Gerry on a trip to Arkansas. To say that was memorable was an understatement, and we put a hurt on them to their surprise. Thirdly, we played burnout with some of the neighborhood boys who happened to be the sons of the local high school coach when we lived in Ft. Worth. Being able to win at burnout with local football stars did not win much chance for any further encounter, but it was great fun!

28 – Verbal Gems and Other Family Treasures

hether at home or somewhere in town or out of town, experiencing verbal gems was a priceless treasure! My sisters made several additions to the family jewelry box.

Terri was not much smaller than I was. She had light, golden-blonde, curly hair, big beautiful blue eyes, and a great big smile. Even as a little child, she was very articulate and confident in conversations. Mom often commented that if a telephone pole stood still long enough, she would talk to it!

We went to the National Grocery Store one day, and Dad left us standing at a turnstile rack of children's books. I was very interested in watching the stars at night, and to my amazement, a book about constellations was displayed. I reached out with great joy, proclaiming that I had found a book on astrology! My learned younger sister quickly corrected me, "That is Astronomy! Not Astrology!" Big difference! She has always been pretty sharp like that.

The evenings in St. Louis were often sweltering in the summer. Before air-conditioned homes and cars became popular, we often hopped into the car to ride around at night to get a little cool air.

Sometimes, we stopped for gas and headed out for a treat at the Dairy Queen® or Chuck-a-Burger®, or we would do a little shopping. It was about the time the Hula Hoops® and Silly Putty® were first sold in stores. I remember getting Hula Hoops® in two different sizes. The larger was used around your waist, and the smaller was used with your arms or even your ankles if you were really adept. That was not me!

On a few occasions, we headed up to the north part of St. Louis County to a kiddie park called Holiday Hills. They had all sorts of rides, and we made our way over to the little boats. We ran up the ramp, and when it was Terri's turn, she stepped out to get into her boat, but instead of stepping into it, she walked right out and into the water.

Dad grabbed her and said, "Honey, why in the world did you do that?"

Startled and soaking wet, she cried, "I thought it was glass!"

It seems to me that it was not long after that Terri got glasses. Kim got hers also.

The St. Louis Zoo in Forest Park was just a few miles from where we lived. Originally it was part of the St. Louis World's Fair in 1904 and is still the best free attraction in the United States. We visited several times and saw many fantastic exhibits and animal shows! On one of our visits, we went to the immense aviary to see the beautifully colored birds from all over the world. We were in awe of the sheer variety. Terri ran toward the cage. In great disbelief and wide eyes, she shouted, "Daddy, Daddy, Daddy, look at that thousand-pound chicken!" upon encountering her first ostrich!

Kim added a totally new dimension to our family. She was six years younger than me and four years younger than Terri. Bouncing was her favorite activity. She often sat on the couch, sang and bounced her back against it continually until she was halfway across the wooden living room floor!

One Easter Sunday, when we arrived home from church, Mom took us into the house and ushered us into the living room. She pulled the heavy sliding wooden door shut to block our view of the front yard. Dad prepared the yard for our Easter egg hunt. In a short while, he came barreling through the kitchen door, yelling, "Where's my shotgun! Where's my shotgun! There's some stupid rabbit laying eggs all over the front yard!!!"

The three of us started screaming, jumped on Dad, trying to hold him back as best as three little girls could! "NO! NO! NO! NO! DADDY! That's the Easter Bunny! Please, Daddy! Please! Don't shoot the Easter Bunny! Please, Daddy, please!" We were all about to break out in tears when he started laughing so hard. He grabbed us all, hugged us, and led us out to the Easter egg hunt!

Mom always picked out the prettiest dresses for us to wear, and Dad manned the home movie camera. He loved following us around as we searched all over the yard. Kim ran so fast to get one colored egg that she accidentally kicked it, and it rolled several feet in front of her! Then she had to run further to try to get it again. Of course, that was caught on film, and every time we viewed that scene, Dad would reverse it so that it looked like the egg was chasing her while she was running backward. Sounds familiar as Dad recorded me doing the same thing several years before. I guess he could not get enough of little girls being chased by eggs.

Summers were no different for us than for many others across the United States when it came to the weekend barbecue. Most of the people who participated in them did so to keep the inside of the houses cooler since most homes were not yet air-conditioned.

On one of those warm Saturday afternoons, Dad and Mom decided to barbecue in our backyard. We had a portable black grill that Dad set up. He filled it with a pile of charcoal, doused it with lighter fluid, and then lit it with a match. He fanned the flames until the charcoal got red hot. I can still remember the strange burning odor wafting through the air. While he was doing that, Mom was in the kitchen wrapping red potatoes, corn on the cob, and whole onions individually in aluminum foil. She made iced tea or her fruit punch and a salad. The chicken was marinated overnight in the refrigerator. Everything needed for the barbecue was taken outside to Dad. I spotted the chicken. To me, it was disgusting because the sauce she used was very spicy, and once the chicken was cooked, it always looked more like a burnt offering than dinner.

I was so frustrated over the matter that I decided I would just run away from home! I went to the toy box to retrieve my red, white, and blue skate case, dumped the skates, and packed my doll and all her clothes, muttering to myself all the way! How dare they try to feed me that disgusting chicken! Well, Mom heard all the racket and went and told Dad what was transpiring. I picked up my case and barreled out the front door! I was so angry that I stomped to the corner and headed west down the street toward the setting sun! I would show them!

Getting about two houses down the street, I turned around to take one more look at my past, and to my surprise, there they were! Standing under my favorite maple tree was my dad, proudly holding my baby sister Kim in his arms and my sister Terri close by his side! I could not believe my eyes! I thought for sure they were worried about me, but no! They were waving goodbye and calling out, "Bye, Zene! Have a good time!" What? Have a good time!?! Are you kidding me!?!

I stomped my feet again and marched with all the determination I could muster down the street past a few more cars. I turned around again, and with more enthusiasm, they yelled to me, "Bye, Zene! Have a good time!" I looked at them in startled disbelief. Turning again, with a broken heart and tears rolling down my face, I managed to walk a little further and ducked behind a big green car. Dropping my skate case on the ground, I slumped down on the rear bumper and cried. Not only did they not care about how much I hated barbecue chicken, but they also did not even care that I was running away from home!!!

I stayed on that bumper for what seemed like ten minutes, and my sister Terri ran up to me! I looked up at her, clearly devastated, and she said, "Dad says, you better come home right now!" I was so embarrassed! I silently thought, "He could not even come and get me himself; he sent Terri!" I could not figure out where to go. Never mind that I was extremely ill-prepared for the journey at age seven or eight. I grudgingly picked up my case and followed her back home! I reached Dad at the corner and looked up at his eyes. It was probably all he could do to keep from bursting out laughing, but he did not. He told me to go back into the house and get ready for dinner.

I said, "Am I going to have to eat barbecue chicken?"

He grinned and said, "Yes!"

To which I replied with a very sad groan!

Throughout Second and Third Grade

29 - Second Grade

Second Grade was filled with new experiences. A different level of maturity was before me, and the support of Miss Palmquist was gone. I entered the classroom, which was darker and less cheerful than first grade. That was mainly due to its location in the building. However, it is something to be noted, that even small children are quite aware of and affected by the appearance of natural light and the way a room feels.

Mrs. Brese was much more a business-like teacher. She taught cursive handwriting and was very resolved that we make each stroke correctly. Her seriousness caused me to strive harder, and I enjoyed it. She did have a strange habit of saving the students' artwork and later slicing them into strips for bookmarks. I was a little crushed when I went to turn in something at her desk and saw her sacrificing one of my prettiest creations!

On a happier note, that year, the primary grades put on the operetta, *The Land of Dreams Come True*. It was the second play in which I participated. In the first one in kindergarten, I was a bluebell. This time, Terri was one of sixteen bluebells, and I was one of sixteen roses. The play was about children going to a land built around nursery rhymes. I must say that we had great fun performing our parts.

Mom, of course, made our costumes from endless yards of blue, red, and green crepe paper. Stacks and stacks of bluebell and rose petals and green leaves were cut out and sewn together in rows to fashion our costumes. She made the cutest hats, which looked like upside-down bluebell buds and rosebuds complete with green stems. They framed our faces allowing for our golden locks to sprawl over our shoulders. She made us look adorable.

Not only did Terri and I become little actresses in the play, but we had our own personal cameraman on the home front. He was anxious to record a dress rehearsal of our dances.

He took his handheld movie camera out and loaded the film. Mom was delegated to hold the floodlight bar complete with a series of four blinding lights to point toward our "action". There was no audio recording in the setup. So then, we were participants of the silent home movies of the 1960s.

Terri put on her bluebell costume, I donned my rose costume, and we met him in the living room for the filming. Dad coaxed us into our places, and Terri seemed to have no problem with her dance. Then, I stepped up to do my part involving an excruciatingly slow dance to the words and music:

> "Mary, Mary, quite contrary,
> How does your garden grow?
> With silver bells and cockle shells
> And pretty maids all in a row!"

Dad tried as he might to cajole us through our motions as quickly as possible. Everyone who knows me is well aware that if I am going to do something, I will start at the beginning and work my way through the entire presentation without skipping a beat. My dance had lots of waving arm movements and slow turning in place. I began singing and waving my arms just the way I was supposed to do for the play. Dad seemed to miss the patience gene altogether. The more he prodded me, the more frustrated we both became. I lost my place and tried to explain that I could not do it quickly and started over. That was not sitting well with Dad. I had no concept of how short a home movie was. He seemed to have no idea of the precision I was affording my presentation!

The whole thing turned out to be a bust, and I do not remember whether the film was ever developed. We got a second chance at a personal performance after school let out for the summer. Our dad's youngest brother, Uncle Porter, visited us over the Memorial Day weekend, bringing his sweet new bride, Aunt Shirley. Again we donned our costumes and gave them a private performance in the front yard. Terri twirled around and around in the quick movements of the bluebell dance. I meticulously moved with much less speed to the waving arm movements of the rose dance with a final slow twirl at the end. It is funny how showing off children to their favorite relatives brings pride and patience to many parents.

To digress a little, the night of the play came, and we all enjoyed the excitement at the school. Each group of actors had their own classroom makeshift dressing rooms and waited, less than patiently, for curtain calls. The halls rang with hushed giggles as we made our way to the gym's back entrance and then onto the brightly lit stage. The students were dressed in all kinds of costumes, including the Old Woman in the Shoe and Little Miss Muffet. I wish now that the whole play would have been read aloud to the students before we did it. That would have been even more fun.

30 - Girl Scouts

While in second grade, I was the first in the family to join the Girl Scouts. In 1961, the beginning level was Brownies. We met once a week at Grace Lutheran Church right after school. This was very convenient for the parents. Every Tuesday, we walked across the street, taking the long sidewalk to the entrance in the back of the church. We met in the basement of the classroom wing.

I loved being a Girl Scout because it gave me a sense of growing up and becoming more responsible. At the Brownie level, we wore little brown dresses with matching socks and brown beanies. Our troop number was 486. Three small darker brown embroidered patches with white numbers were sewn onto the uniforms. We wore two pins: one which stood for the Brownie motto and the other the Girl Scout Trefoil. We were taught about being good citizens and how to be honorable and helpful. We learned the motto and the pledge.

"The Girl Scout Motto"

Be Prepared.

"The Girl Scout Pledge"

On my honor,
I will try to do my duty,
To God and my country,

To help other people at all times,
And to obey the Girl Scout laws.

Songs were crucial to the life of a Girl Scout, and we learned an abundance of them. Singing was right up my alley, and during my six years in scouts, each new song filled another page in my memories.

Following are several of those songs:

"The Happy Wanderer"

I love to go a-wandering,
Along the mountain track,
And as I go, I love to sing,
My knapsack on my back.

Chorus

Val-deri,
Val-dera,
Val-deri,
Val-dera-ha-ha-ha-ha-ha
Val-deri,Val-dera.
My knapsack on my back.

Verse 2

I wave my hat to all I meet,
And they wave back to me,
And blackbirds call so loud and sweet
From ev'ry green wood tree.

Repeat chorus

Verse 3

Oh, may I go a-wandering
Until the day I die!
Oh, may I always laugh and sing,
Beneath God's clear blue sky[3,4]!

Repeat chorus:

"Hey Ho, Nobody Home"

Hey ho, nobody home
Meat nor drink nor money have I none
Yet I will be merry
Hey ho, nobody home...

Repeat a lot and also in rounds!"Make New Friends"
(sung in rounds)

Make new friends and keep the old
One is silver and the other's gold.

I loved the truth of these rich and full words. Behind it is adventure and stability. Adding my smile that wells up from my toes (a beautiful gift from God) has opened many doors I never could have imagined.

"Three Blue Pigeons", "Agnamena, Magdamena", "There's a Hole in the Bucket", "The Ants Go Marching", and "Oh, Plant a Watermelon" were songs that were usually accompanied by tons of laughter among the girls. If sung too often at home, they could get on the last nerve of a tired parent. So, one would have to choose carefully the appropriate time to sing them. And on and on and on!

All the songs we learned increased our camaraderie, which was a delightful effect. If I ran into any of my old friends from scouts, I could easily break out a hint of the old songs. Immediately, we would pick up where we left off. This, too, is a sweet gift.

Just as important as the music of Girl Scouts was the making of crafts! The excitement of creating something new and usable was birthed early in my life. Each item we learned to make was planted in the fertile field of imagination. Those seeds produce blooms, and fruit in future creations. I thrived in these activities.

We made "sit-upons" to use for sitting on the floor in a circle. They were two square pieces of vinyl with holes punched all the way around and stuffed with a piece of foam, then laced. Dad and Mom hand punched holes in all that vinyl for two Girl Scout troops. They used a tool that looked a little like a pair of pliers having a cog on one end with variable-sized hole punchers. I know they were totally worn out after punching several hundred holes for that project. The girls were all too little to do the punching themselves. Another laced project was television guide covers. In those days, *TV Guide* was a trendy magazine that listed the programs for television stations for a week at a time. During those years, there were only three or four stations available. *TV Guide* is still being published and is easily obtained at grocery and chain stores.

We made hot pads from canning jar rubber rings and yarn. For another project, we took two tiles and four small matchboxes. We glued them together, transforming them into a match storage and strike station for coffee tables. Large water goblets were turned into Christmas candy jars with felt faces, and red felt hats. Ornaments were made from glittered milkweed pods and unshelled walnuts. Decorative candles resulted from pouring melted wax into milk cartons filled with a tapered candle and crushed ice. When the wax cooled, the cartons were torn away, and water poured from the holes left by the crushed ice. Another beautiful wax creation involved pouring hot wax into a bucket of swirling water.

Ditty bags were fun to make. Small lengths of fabric were sewn together and filled with toiletry items. These were taken to Altenheim for gifts for the elderly residents.

We adopted grandparents at least for that visit and got to spend some personal time with them. Some of the girls kept up with their "grandparents" after that trip, which was very rewarding. My "grandmother" was a sweet lady who was blind. She was very gracious and showed me her braille books. They were fascinating.

From that visit, I was encouraged to learn about the famous blind woman named Helen Keller. I read a book about her life named *The Miracle Worker*. Later on we were able to view the movie. It was a compelling film about a marvelous sight-impaired woman named Anne Sullivan. In her incredible dedication, she led Helen not to live like a wild animal, but learn to love, be loved, and to speak and eventually live a very fulfilling life. It is remarkable how each encounter with a new person provides a chance to learn something. Sometimes those meetings influence a life for years.

Among the activities in Girl Scouts were fundraisers. The two carried out every year by all of the troops were selling Girl Scout Cookies® and Girl Scout Calendars®. In the early 60s, the cookies sold for fifty cents. Flavors available were Chocolate Mints, now known as Thin Mints, shortbread known as Scot Teas and Peanut Butter Sandwich Cookies. Eventually, the price was raised to seventy-five cents. I have to say, I struggled with selling the cookies at the higher price. My knowledge of economics fell short of understanding price increases. I felt like I was taking advantage of my customers, which gave me a guilty conscience. Maybe my mom's frugality influenced my high sensitivity to the cost of things.

31 – Delaware Avenue

$\mathcal{M}$rs. Weber had a little mom-and-pop grocery store on the corner of Delaware Avenue and Wagner Avenue, one block south of our house. I think she was a widow. She lived in the second story above the store. By the time Terri was in school, our school bus had begun picking us up right across the street from Mrs. Weber's. If we left early enough, Mom gave us a little money to spend for Smith Brothers®, Ludens®, or Sucrets® cough drops when we had colds. We made our purchases and dropped them into our little purses.

Other times, Mom took us there for treats. She picked up an empty soda bottle carton, and we went to the cooler, and each of us selected our favorite soda. The six flavors picked were orange, grape, black cherry, Mountain Dew®, and two Pepsi®. Sometimes she let us choose bakery treats. My favorite was Hostess Snowball Cupcakes®. They were dome-shaped chocolate cake covered with pink or white marshmallow frosting dipped in coconut. Terri enjoyed Hostess Chocolate Cupcakes®, while Hostess Twinkies® delighted us with long tubes of yellow cake. All three treats had some whipped cream in the center. Wonder Bread®, Miracle Whip®, and Hellmann's Mayonnaise® for making sandwiches often made their way to the grocery bag.

Other than Mrs. Weber herself, the biggest treat was her enticing candy counter right by the front door! For twenty-five cents, we could get a small bag of our own choices of the candies. She also carried pretzel rods. I always got at least five of them. Black Cows® were hard thin rectangular caramels on sticks dipped in chocolate. Kits®, Sweetarts®, taffies, malted milk balls, and lollipops were other choices. We spent many hours in Mrs. Weber's store.

Mom got her hair done at a beauty shop on Delaware Avenue. About the summer of the fourth grade, a new hairstyle called teasing became the rage among women. Many of them went to beauty parlors more often to get their hair done than doing it themselves. They carefully wrapped scarves over their hairdos before they went to bed to keep them neat for as long as a week. At that point, Mom got even pickier about anyone touching her hair. She also decided that year to let us get short haircuts. It was cooler for us, but I think Dad would have rather let us keep our long hair. Dad decided to join in with his own change. For a long time, he sported a skinny mustache, which he shaved it off on one of his trips. It completely escaped our notice for six weeks. He could not believe it and was pretty disheartened by our oversight.

We spent hours and hours skating on the sidewalks in our front and back yards. The skates were made entirely of metal parts with a leather strap to tie them around our ankles. A specially designed key was used to adjust the clamps to adapt them to our shoe sizes. If not tightened enough, they flopped off, making it easy to trip and fall. They were quite sufficient to get the gist of skating so that when we rented skates at the roller rink, we could get around with a little more confidence. One early evening Dad took us across the street to skate in the front parking area of the used car lot after it closed for the day. We were having a great time as Kim chased after us in the bouncy run of a toddler. She was all the while trying to hang on to my favorite red pouch purse. That purse had a little history. Once, I accidentally left it on the back porch during a rainstorm. A stack of graham crackers was in it, and that made a pretty sloppy soup to clean up. The first blind reach inside was pretty gross. Kim enjoyed that purse as much as I did.

Dad and Mom decided to get a bicycle for me and tricycles for Terri and Kim. Because I was the oldest, Mom, in her thrifty mode, prevailed upon Dad not to waste money on a bike for my actual size. So he brought home one that I could barely get on and stay on even when it was still. He wheeled it to Delaware Avenue beside our house and took it on a test drive. Then he persuaded me to get on, and he would hold onto it and run beside me while I peddled. Warily, I mounted the bike, and off we went down the block turning the corner at Wagner Avenue next to Mrs. Weber's store. At that time, Wagner Avenue was only one block long west from Delaware. It sloped down to the dead-end where a good four-feet or five-feet drop landed one into a creek filled with crayfish. Things were going okay until Dad decided to let go so I could experience going down the slope. My speed increased, and I cried out to Dad, who at that point was not beside me.

"Slow me down, slow me down, stop, stop, stop!" My cries were to no avail, and there I was facing imminent danger!

In the excitement of teaching his daughter to ride a bike, Dad failed to provide one crucial piece of information: how to use the brakes! Fearing the dilemma of landing in the creek with the crayfish, the only option I could think of was to fall off the bike on the road. Fall I did, very hard onto the asphalt getting badly scraped up. He could not believe his eyes! I could not believe that he had done that to me! I did not have a clue what brakes were, that I had them, or even how to use them! The bike and I wrestled with each other for several weeks before I became its master. I learned then that an introduction to a new skill made complete instructions quite invaluable!

On a gorgeously sunny Sunday afternoon in August, when the grass was a luscious green and the sky was a crystal blue, Dad was enticed to pull out his movie camera. He gathered us outside after we returned from church to record our abilities on wheels.

Still in our purple, green and red dresses, Terri and Kim mounted the two tricycles, and I took to the bicycle. Our smiles were from ear to ear. Kim was still too little to peddle, so Mom stepped on the back of her tricycle and pushed her down the walkway. It was kind of funny as Mom was wearing a slim fit black dress with a boat neckline that did not give her much room to move. Then Kim got off and just started dragging it around. Dad pulled, and I pushed Terri and Kim in the wagon. Kim commandeered it for use as a gravel hauler filling it with rocks one by one. Terri raced against me with her tricycle, and then more action was recorded in the backyard with the swing set and slide. Then we went back to the street side of the house just as two of Dorothy's sons, Mike and Ron, came walking by. It was memorable because Mike had recently joined the army and was wearing his new uniform. Ron waved, but Mike saluted my dad as they passed. Just then, Dad jumped onto my bicycle, which for me was too big, but his frame caused him to look like a giant. Back and forth, he rode, pretending to do tricks and driving with no hands. His legs bent out to the sides, making him look like an airplane coming in for a landing. He looked so funny wearing his black business hat and slacks, white shirt, and tie, as he peddled standing up. I am sure a good lunch and naps followed all these activities.

32 - Third Grade

he great thing about third grade was that each student at Concord Lutheran School was required to have their own personal Holy Bible and a book called *Growing in Christ*. That was an exciting step! Mom gathered us together, and we made a trip by the city bus to Concordia Publishing House at the corner of Jefferson and Miami. (This had been the business' location since 1874). I was in total awe of the place lined with more books than I had ever seen before.

Mom picked up a white Bible with a zippered cover and took it to the counter to have it embossed with our last name! She gave the Bible to the three of us girls collectively. When I went to school carrying our new Holy Bible (King James Version) with our last name on it and my *Growing in Christ*, I felt like I was at the beginning of a great adventure, and I was! I cherish all that I have learned from both of those books. These many years, I spend time reading the Bible nearly every day and am still amazed at what I learn from the teachings.

On another trip to Concordia Publishing House, Mom bought copies of *The Lutheran Hymnal* in the new red edition for Terri and me and had our names embossed on them. I cannot begin to tell you how many precious moments were gained in the thousands of hours poured over the hymns.

Third grade was also a stressful time for me. The teacher was a little tense as she was expecting and due at the end of the school year. The room was painted a dismal green color adding to its joylessness.

I remember being teased and bullied. One morning, it was my turn to be the lunchroom monitor for our class's table. Still being slight of build, shy, and possessing a little bit of a legalistic mindset, things did not turn out well for me. After making the usual report after lunch, I was lined up with those I reported and given a smack on the hand with a ruler. Later one of the girls cornered me in the hallway and chewed me out. After the teacher had disciplined me, there was no way I was going to get help from her. I still do not have a clue as to why I was punished.

The weather contributed to the stress I felt that year. One afternoon, while seated in the classroom, we watched the sky turn that sick green color which prophecies possible tornadoes. It was nerve-racking to see the winds and rain churn the clouds so threateningly. Alas, no tornado was reported, but the sight was unforgettable. In the back of some of our minds was the devastating tornado which hit St. Louis in February of 1959. Twenty-one fatalities and three hundred forty-five injuries occurred in that storm, and we were all old enough to have some memory of it. A good portion of the arena's roof was torn away, and seeing the pictures made many of us very wary of these fierce storms.

It seemed that third grade was the time for me to contract measles and mumps, so as many other students missed school days, so did I. Pink-eye and an infected tooth added no comfort.

By spring, I was sporting braces. My adult teeth erupted through my gums in the disorderliness of new untrained recruits in the military. They had no intention of lining up correctly without insistence. There were a few very positive outcomes. Because the process began at such an early time in my life, my gums were quite malleable. My dentist and my parents were greatly surprised within six unbelievably short weeks. Indeed, the blessing of straight pearly whites enabled the graduation from dental boot camp. Unfortunately, it was determined that I had a calcium deficiency, which contributed to the need for some fillings in my back teeth. I was very grateful when the process was complete and had no problem eating or breaking out in a beaming smile afterward.

Arkansas

33 – Going to Grandma's

A summer never passed without a seven-hour road trip to Searcy, Arkansas, to visit relatives. The further south we drove, the more hilly it was as we reached the Ozarks' northeastern edge. This activity became a joyously anticipated highlight of the ride to Grandma's house, especially with Kim! Dad loved to drive as fast as safely possible to the peaks so that when we headed down the other side of the mountains, our stomachs would feel like they were continuing the ascent. Kim named the new family sport, "Tummy Bouncing"! Seeing each steep incline as the next target, she gleefully pleaded with Dad to go faster. He would try to accommodate her. The cheers and laughter made the trips more and more fun-filled. Afterward, we made a quick pitstop in Poplar Bluff, Missouri. Then, crossing the state line, we passed many water-filled rice fields. The contrast between the green plants and the blue sky reflections on the interlaced irrigation ditches was a beautiful sight.

We always stayed with Grandma while we were in Arkansas, and her house became a sort of base of operations. Before 1962, 800 North Main Street was the last home on the road going north from the center of town. When my sisters and I were very young, it felt like Grandma's house was the last hold of civilization between the fair city and the wild country and farming areas. The stark paradox was cemented in our hearts by the land's appearance on the north side of the house in its neglected and natural state. Massive old trees from which no leaf had sprung since long ago produced quite an eerie view in the light of a full moon. The mist from the nearby creek, enhancing the foreboding feeling, was quite enough to keep us from wandering off of her property. Today that paradoxical memory is quite amusing given the fact that Grandma lived only five blocks from the courthouse in the city square and not seven blocks from the city park. Harding College was less than a mile away. The perception and imagination of young minds are quite vivid, to say the least.

The reality of being at Grandma's house was a wonderfully stark contradiction to the first impression of the previous paragraph. It was a sweet-looking white wood-framed house with an attached carport and a gravel driveway. A large tree and several bushes stood in the front yard. The house had large wood-framed windows on the front and a generous porch from the front door toward the carport.

One year she had some white four o'clock vines hanging from the roof of the porch. Grandma called us outside in the early evening to behold the opening of the blossoms. Each petal's movement was graceful and perceptible to anyone who took the time to enjoy their beauty. They remained open all night and closed early the next morning. It was so impressive and better than anything that we could see on our television at home. In fact, I do not remember Grandma ever owning a television.

Sweet potato vines that she had tacked up along the living room's entire perimeter welcomed us as we came through the front door. I think that Dad felt like we were entering a jungle. There was a couch that could be used as a bed by the window next to the carport and a beautiful old upright piano on the opposite wall. No one was allowed to play it, and it was usually kept locked. The dining area and Grandma's bedroom were side by side. She had a dresser with a large mirror. Her rouge lay neatly with her other personal items. I always wanted to try it on but did not, although I did open it to see what it looked like. Dad used to tell us how Grandma once had a dresser that she demolished with an ax because she found a snake in it!

There was a gas heater in the dining room, which was the house's sole heat source. A big round old wooden table stood in quiet testimony to thousands of meals and held the memories of family times over decades of use. Sadly, Mom and Dad bought Grandma a more modern formica kitchen table similar to the one we owned, but I always loved the old wooden table more. Her refrigerator was also in the dining room.

There was a narrow kitchen at the back of the house, with the bathroom on the left and the screened-in porch on the right. (She kept a ton of African violets out there on that old wooden dining table which was relegated to the back porch). Grandma loved African violets! In fact, she loved them so much that they were all over the house, and it became a chief activity on each trip to count the plants. Our Dad had no love for the over-abundance of flowers, and dis-affectionately referred to them as Grandma's "weeds."

A broad white porcelain sink with an ample wooden counter on the left of it and a gas stove on the right was anchored underneath a row of wood-framed windows, which provided a great view of a sunny backyard and her clotheslines. It was a beautiful sight when the skies were a bright blue. The walls were a warm buttery yellow.

The bathroom was off to the left of the kitchen. It had a big white cast-iron tub with clawed feet and an old water heater and commode. We loved that tub because the back end was sloped like an inviting water slide. It compelled any young user to mount its ledge and slide into the pool of warm water. None of us got away with that activity more than once, as it caused the contents to be hurled in a wave over the edge of the tub and inconveniently soak the floor, making a huge mess. Once per person was a sweet memory, though.

A second door from the bathroom led to another small kitchen. A door from that little kitchen led out to the field where those scary trees stood! Beside that kitchen, going toward the front of the house was the second bedroom. It was very roomy, and in the daytime, bright, cheery sunlight poured through the front windows. I remember the bare-bulbed electric lights in the house hanging from the ceiling. They were operated with pull chains rather than light switches on the walls. The bedroom also had one of those doors that was cut in half crossways from side to side. The top half could be opened while leaving the bottom half shut. This door led back to the living room. I remember thinking the bedroom would have been a welcoming place to sleep except for the scary trees outside and the fact that the house was the last one on the road leaving town.

34 – Grandma and the Family

Grandma was 5'7" tall and thin and had white, curly, neatly arranged hair. She always wore dresses, no matter where she was going or what she was doing. Her terrific smile and giggle complimented her blues eyes that sparkled when she was happy. However, it was hard to get her to smile for a picture as she did not like her teeth, but over the years, a few great shots were preserved for the family. She was rather quiet and seemed more interested in enjoying the others' conversations, serving, and watching everyone. Even so, I knew that she loved me all the same by the hugs and smiles I got from her. She was the only one I knew that called Dad, "James," and the tone in her voice instantly identified that he was her son.

Grandma was very active in her Methodist Church. We always visited there with her when we were in town. It was a lovely little red brick building with Sunday School classes in rooms behind the sanctuary. Grandma lived out her faith but did not share much about it with us. Though I somehow felt that she prayed a lot for us all.

Besides her love for flowers, she loved sewing. She made most of her clothes and also recycled her old clothing to make quilts. Grandma was the seamstress making alterations for customers at a clothing store in downtown Searcy. The store was across the street from the courthouse in the town square. Sometimes she was still at work when we arrived in town. We met up with her just before she got off. She came out from her little room at the side of the dressing area, wearing a tape measure over her neck, ready for the next alteration. I loved meeting her at her work because she got the biggest smile on her face and was so proud to introduce us to her fellow employees. In the center of the store was a very wide wooden staircase to the second floor that was so inviting. I dare not succumb to the temptation to race up and down its steps because we needed to behave respectfully and quietly while there. Once she finished, we were off to her house for our time with her.

Grandma was an excellent cook! She made the best homemade biscuits and had a yeast roll recipe that produced the best yeast rolls that just melted in your mouth! Her secret recipe was only shared with one other person: her youngest son. She loved making peanut brittle and always tried to make a banana cake for Dad while we were there. Her beef stew was excellent! On a few occasions, the family got together for a big fish fry with the fresh fish the men caught during the day. Grandma could fry the best mess of fish ever, complete with cornbread, fried okra, beefsteak tomatoes from her garden, and corn on the cob! After the meal, the aunts and the girl cousins headed to the kitchen for cleanup duty. She made an ice cream mixture for homemade ice cream. When it was ready, the men's privilege was to go out to the carport and take turns churning until it hardened. A few big watermelons were chilled in a galvanized tub filled with ice. Some of the family, including Dad, loved to put salt on their watermelon when served. A buzz was in the air as we all enjoyed each other's company in the late glow of a setting sun!

Terri recently remarked about how she thinks of those days long ago, chatting with the ladies around the kitchen chores. There was always a lot of laughter and teasing going on. Of course, someone was constantly yelling out, "Stop slamming the screen doors, you are letting in all the flies!" as children ran in and out of the house! In the futility of fighting the slamming of doors, each child was armed with a flyswatter and sent in to fight the flies. We quickly learned the boundaries of where a battle was allowed or not allowed. At all costs, we were not to swat flies as they landed on any food.

Dad snuck in one fishing trip with Terri and me at a river while we were in Arkansas. We were probably six and eight at the time. He rented a boat, and we loaded it up with the bait, poles, gear, lures, and lunch, and up the river, he paddled. It was our first time in a boat. The water was green and murky looking. We fished for several hours, and when it was time to go, Dad rowed the boat back to the dock carrying the eight fish I caught and the eleven fish Terri caught. We were left with the gear as he went for the car. Terri still had bait on her pole, so she kept on fishing. All of a sudden, her line was snagged, and she struggled with all her might to try to drag that fish in! When Dad heard the commotion, he turned and saw his younger daughter being dragged to the dock's edge, but she, with the strength of David fighting Goliath, was not about to give in! He screamed out, "TERRI, LET GO OF THE POLE!" "NO, DADDY!" was her determined cry! Reaching her just before the fish could pull her off the dock and into the river, he grabbed her and helped her pull in a considerably large gar! He immediately released it as gars are very vicious and dangerous! They are prehistoric-looking predator fish with long snouts like alligators, and their mouths are loaded with razor-sharp needle-like teeth! Dad assured us that it was best to let it go and informed us that they were not edible. Terri was crushed to lose her prey, but we were all glad we did not lose her! He was so very proud of her!

When we got back to grandma's house, we were sporting nineteen fish. Dad was bursting with pride even though he had not caught a single one! He strutted around the house like a rooster brandishing the day's stories and his excitement over Terri's experience! It was indeed a great story of "the one that got away"!

We visited several relatives, including Grandma's brother Lyman and her sister Jessie at their farms in the White County area. Her sister Anna May ran the little grocery store in West Point. She was also the postmistress there. Each visit brought new experiences to us, and we were always welcomed with joy and laughter. The West Point Cemetery was on the list to visit family gravesites. Drives further out in the country allowed us to see where Dad grew up. I enjoyed meeting Grandma's siblings and their families and seeing how they lived.

We spent Memorial Day weekend at Grandma's in May of 1961. While there, we took a trip to see Aunt Virginia and Uncle Harold, cousins Gerry, Sheila, and Monie. They lived across from the high school where Uncle Harold was a teacher. Grandma, Uncle Henry, and Aunt Doris and her twin brother, Uncle Bill, Uncle Porter, and his new bride, Aunt Shirley, all attended. Late in the afternoon, Dad recorded all the family antics, including jumping rope, for the action. It was not quite normal to see adults jump rope, but lots of fun as the craziness progressed.

Afterward, we drove to see where one of the major roads had washed out due to massive flooding. A large metal and wooden bridge was still intact but only led to a completely submerged road on the other side. It was a sad and frightening sight and hard for me to understand how that could happen. There were several casualties from floods across the United States that year.

A few other sites we visited were a place called Sugar Loaf, where there is this mountain in a field that looks like it has an enormous loaf of bread on the top of it. Aunt Doris and Uncle Henry lived in Little Rock. Greers Ferry Lake was the destination for a picnic and swimming trip. Grandma could not swim but managed to wade out in the water to about ten inches deep, holding the skirt of her dress up just enough to keep it from getting wet. She was pretty cute, standing there watching the rest of us thoroughly enjoying playing in the water.

In July, Dad had to make a business trip to Memphis and decided to take us with him. The fact that we were close enough to make a side trip to see Grandma afforded us another opportunity to swing by and spend some time with family. Again, all were coerced to perform in the front yard. This time "London Bridge is Falling Down" was the theme, and children and adults alike participated. We had gotten more used to our director's cues, and the acting was much more natural and enjoyable. The twinkle in Grandma's eyes testified to the delight in watching so many in her family at play together. She even entered the bridge with a great big smile on her face. Kim was picked up and passed around from one relative to another and enjoying each exchange. The movie filmed provided many more close-ups of family members, and that is a precious gift from a time gone by.

In August, we took a vacation to Lake Wappapello, Missouri. We camped in a cabin and swam in the lake while Dad fished in a boat. He was eagerly looking forward to the solitude, but we hated watching him row away. We all would have preferred that he stay with us, but that was just the way it was, and there was no changing his mind. I think he just hated swimming. I only saw him in swim trunks twice in my life. One evening after a successful catch, the men at the camp gathered at a work table constructed for cleaning their prizes. It was the first time I saw fish scaled and filleted. A man asked me if I wanted to help, and I declined. He laughed. We spent several days on the lake and then went on to Searcy.

Aunt Doris invited us to see The Old Mill, located at T. R. Pugh Memorial Park in North Little Rock. It is a re-creation of a water-powered grist mill from the 1880s and was built in 1933 when my dad was just nine years old. Opening scenes of the movie Gone With

The Wind were filmed there. It was great walking with Grandma and Aunt Doris around the mill and the bridge that looked like it was built of boulders and gnarled tree limbs.

One of our favorite things was to spend time with our cousins Sheila and Monie. Sheila tells the story that if they got there before we were awake, they were not allowed to get us up. Now that just was not right! I mean, are you kidding? If we had realized when they were coming, we probably would not have slept at all!

In 1962, the property next door to Grandma's was bought by the Downtown Church of Christ. All the trees were cleared for the new church building, and we saw the progress of the sanctuary construction. I had just finished fifth grade when we headed down to Searcy for one of our visits. Cousins Sheila and Monie were also coming, and we were so excited. We were stair steps in age, Sheila being the oldest, then me, then Monie, then Terri. We were like the Four Musketeers when we were together. I decided to share my newly acquired science knowledge with the group, fully intending to impress them with the names of the types of rock formations I had studied. Taking advantage of the fact that large gravel had been recently laid in the driveway of the churchyard next door, Sheila marched us over and picked up a rock and most assuredly announced to us, "THIS, is a boot rock!" I looked at her in amazement. I was not about to contradict one of my most admired cousins! We had not studied any rock forms named boot rocks before, but if Sheila said it was a boot rock, it was indeed a boot rock, and that settled the matter!

As adults forty-some years later, Sheila and her mother, our Aunt Virginia, visited us in Florida. I asked her if she remembered the "boot rock" story, and she told me that she did not. When I recalled the incident fully to her, her face turned red as she laughed out loud and said to me, "Well, if I said that it was a 'boot rock,' then it was a 'boot rock!'" I giggled and said to her, "Why yes! If Sheila said it, it must be so!" This episode has since been recalled on many occasions as the sister cousin relationships have grown over these years. It is a beautiful thing when your cousins continue to be some of your dearest and best friends even though you only spent a few times a year together.

Every visit came to a close way too soon, and we usually headed home after a good breakfast at Grandma's house. We gave our hugs and kisses and took our places in the car. Even now, the ache of leaving her waving goodbye to us from the driveway causes me to hold back tears. There was so much more I wish I could have experienced with her. Living three-hundred miles away was a hard barrier to overcome!

Wings and Chariots

35 - Airplane Trip

Occasionally Dad's work trips required him to travel by airplane. He had a speaking engagement in Memphis, Tennessee, and when he arrived, they could not find his luggage! He was to speak that evening and had to find a store that could sell him a suit, and also alter it right away. At that time, Dad wore a size 44 jacket, but he needed slacks with a size 34" waist and a 36" inseam. The clerk was able to find the suit with a jacket that fit perfectly, but the slacks were way too big for him! The alterationist got busy right away, but the only thing he could do in that short a period of time was to take the slacks in several inches, and that meant that the back pockets wound up being sewn together! Dad did not have any other choice and had to take that remedy! They were barely able to finish in time for Dad to arrive at the meeting to give his speech. From then on, he carried on his luggage rather than having it stowed beneath the plane.

TWA (TransWorld Airlines) and AA (American Airlines) were two of the most popular airlines flying out of Lambert Airport in St. Louis. These were the days before commercial jets were available. Sometimes Mom got us dressed up, and we would go by bus to the airport for Dad's arrival home. It was very exciting to go to the airport and all the way to the gate to meet him! We could watch the planes land from the large windows and see them taxi to the gates.

Being close enough to see the propellers still spinning was amazing to us. Once the plane stopped at the gate, the mobile stairway was pushed to the doors for the passengers to disembark. We peered through the window for the first glimpse of our Dad! Once he made his way into the building and free from the crowd, we all but tackled him in the terminal with lots of hugs and kisses! After getting his luggage, we headed for the parking area to find his car. There were absolutely no sounds of silence for Dad as each of us vied for his attention.

Dad always had a sweet little custom that he would go through when he arrived home after he had traveled by plane. He gathered his three little girls either in the front room by the radiator or in the living room. He presented us each with packages of neatly wrapped sugar cubes and then placed a cigar band from special cigars he had smoked on our ring fingers. He made a big to do in presenting us each with the tokens of love. Financially, they were not worth much, but the exercise of that precious exchange was a treasure to his daughters.

36 - Dad's Cars

Because my dad traveled so much, he was given the option of using a company car or getting an allowance to buy his own car. He took the second option, so we had a new car every other year.

Dad purchased a green 1961 Ford Fairlane 500. One evening he left the building to come home, and when he went to where he parked his car, it was gone! It turned out that another employee was given the keys to an identical green Ford in the parking lot to go on a business trip. Unfortunately, the keys fit both cars, and the man did not realize he had taken Dad's! Of course, there were no cell phones in 1961, and the only way you could reach a traveler was to call their destination and get a message to them! It was quite a distance away and took a few days for the man to return the car. Besides all that, it was complicated by the fact that the mistake was made at the start of a weekend, making it harder to contact anyone at his destination.

Not long after that ordeal, Dad decided not to purchase a fleet vehicle, but to apply the allowance to a car of his own choosing. So the green car was to become a trade-in. It was time to pick up this new purchase, and Dad took Terri and me to the dealership. We parked inside the service building and went to complete the transactional paperwork. When the keys were exchanged, and it was time to leave, Dad excitedly took us by the hand to the new beautiful two-toned chestnut red 1962 Ford Fairlane 500. Well, Terri took one look at it and immediately tried with all her might to pull our father away from it! "No, Daddy, this is not our car!" He began to explain that we had a new car now, but she would not have any of it! She started crying. Dad got down on one knee and looked at her as comfortingly as he could. He said, "Terri, we have to get this new car and leave the old green one here!" She looked into his eyes with tears rolling down her face, and whimpered, "Why, Daddy?" As sincerely as he could, he explained, "Honey, we have to leave it here because it would not drink its milk!" She sadly grabbed his hand, and he led us away to the new car. Hopefully, this one would drink its milk! I know Terri, and I had no problem drinking ours after that!

We picked this car up from the dealership just before Christmas. The next weekend some of the married couples from the church had a New Year's Eve party in one of their homes. Before the party was over, three big crashes were heard from the street. Upon investigation, it was found that a drunk driver had plowed into not one but three cars parked along the road, one right after the other! He did not realize what he had done in his inebriated state, and kept on driving down the road, leaving a transmission fluid trail behind him. The local police were able to apprehend the passed out driver and asked if he knew he had crashed into three cars. He muttered that he was not aware of it. One officer replied, "You could not have hit anything much newer!

The next morning, the new Fairlane was towed to our driveway. Dad and Mom took us out to see the damage. It was totaled! The driver's side was crushed so severely that the front wheel was nearly torn off and dangled from a shred of metal. What a shock! It kind of makes you wonder. Maybe Dad should have listened to Terri even if the green car would not drink its milk! Only God knows! A few weeks later, Dad was able to get an identical replacement.

At the end of 1963, we were taken to a very fancy Chevrolet dealership in the St. Louis area. Dad wanted to special order a 1964 Palomar Red Chevrolet Impala with an 8-cylinder engine, black interior, and silver satin trim on the sides and back. He called the color Candy Apple Red. We girls looked around the showroom of Placke Chevrolet on South Kingshighway. While we waited, one of the salesmen presented gifts to all the "ladies" in the family. We were given small perfume bottles shaped like flattened crowns and packaged in elegant black boxes! Of course, that made each of us each feel like royalty! Dad finished his order complete with specific instructions to "in no way" mount a dealership advertising plate on the car! He was extremely insistent on those instructions.

The car finally arrived, and we picked it up as a family. It was a gorgeous vehicle! When we went to church the next Sunday, one of the ushers laughingly commented on Rogers' red fire engines, because this was his third red car! That tickled Dad!

I have a lot of great memories of that car and the trips we took in it! Dad all but crushed my heart when he sold it in 1965 to an airline stewardess from Dallas, Texas. I could not believe that he would not keep that car until I was old enough to drive it!

Dad took great pride in all of his cars and always kept them immaculately clean. We never ate in them or brought anything with us that could accidentally make a mess.

Since Dad was the only male in the family, bathroom breaks were often viewed as inconveniences to him. His need to arrive at our destination in record time trumped calls of nature. We were repeatedly told to hold it; we only have about "x" miles to go. Mom tried to appease him by bringing a toddler's potty with us on one trip so that if there was a need, she could hold one of us as we relieved ourselves. It seemed like a plan. In those days, we did not have air conditioning in the cars. Therefore, the wind rushed through the windows weaving loose locks of hair into tangled knots.

Seat belts and car seats were futuristic inventions, and passengers had a lot more freedom to move around the inside of the vehicles.

We were flying low down the highway at record speed when the potty plan was enlisted. My little sister was the first candidate to initiate the plan. When she finished, Mom put the pot on the floor in front of her and helped my sister settle back in her place. Dad said, "I'll slow down a little, and you can empty the pot." So when no traffic was in sight, Dad slowed down to about 50 miles per hour, and Mom picked that pot up from the floor and stuck it out of the window. Instead of turning it away from the wind, she tried to pour out the contents against the wind causing a massive spray to return to the car's cabin. All passengers received a dousing, and Dad was hot! Mom was not any happier than he was, and the battle raged for several miles into a deafening silence.

Lesson learned:
Have girls, will stop, ... at least occasionally!

37 - Business and Family Trip

ad wore out plenty of tire tread with his position working for American Casualty Insurance Company. His territory included Missouri and its eight circuitous neighbors, Illinois, Iowa, Nebraska, Kansas, Oklahoma, Arkansas, Tennessee, and Kentucky.

With a business call to make in Peoria, Illinois late in the week, he took the opportunity to bring us with him. The downtown was lovely. The hotel rooms had tall walls and windows above the doors that could be opened to the hallway for ventilation. The room was picturesque of hotels from the 1920s with ornately woven hallway carpets and polished bronze fixtures and lights. The stay granted the comforts of home and ended with a breakfast of freshly made waffles oozing with melted butter and warm maple syrup, the scent of which wafted through the air like a gentle hug. Drinking orange juice from chilled glasses, distracted my attention from the noise of chatter and clinking dishes and silverware.

The adventure was extended with the completion of Dad's business meeting. For the sake of making good time and distance, meals and bathroom breaks were limited to extreme necessity. Dad was known to jest that his girls knew every bathroom from St. Louis south to Searcy and east to the Atlantic Ocean. However, that was not entirely true. We may have suspected their locations but rarely met with their acquaintance. Just as the sun was teasing its disappearance, Dad spotted a very popular Big Boy Restaurant. We wearily yet hastily abandoned our chestnut red chariot and entered the crisply air-conditioned establishment. Their fish sandwiches and French fries were favorites and could not be brought to the table quickly enough. Dad allowed ample time for deserts of ice cream or hot fudge sundaes, which Mom was ever so delighted in eating. She always insisted on having "slithered" (sliced) almonds added in lieu of peanuts. The thought of that term still makes me smile, and yes, they do add to the treat!

Next, we stopped at Kokomo, Indiana. I think that is an interesting name for a city and fun to roll over your tongue! Dad's cousin Beth and her family lived there. They took us to the visitor's center in Highland Park. To our amazement, Kokomo had on display a real stuffed bull named "Old Ben"! He had been there since 1919. Records show that he was well over 4,500 pounds, stood 6 1/2 feet tall at the shoulder, was 14 feet around his belly and back, and 16 1/4 feet from nose to his tail tip! That was some bull!

Cousin Beth had a boy, Jerry, and a girl, Frances. They taught us to play a game called *Concentration,* which was fashioned after a television show by the same name. They gifted us with our own copy of the game when we left. It was the first board game we had ever owned. We were so excited as Mom and Dad had never taken the time to play games with us before. Soon after that trip, we acquired a game called *Password,* which also was fashioned after a television show by the same name. Terri and I spent long hours laughing and playing both of these games.

38 - Return to the East - Vacation 1962

*I*n July of 1962, we packed the trunk of the Fairlane 500 for vacation and drove to Cleveland, Ohio. Holiday Inn® was our accommodations for the night. Kim called it "Hodiday Inns," which we all thought was pretty cute. It had very large pools and a kiddie pool. Mom bought us clover purple plaid swimsuits, and we could not wait to use them. Swimming was not something we ever had a chance to do at home. I know I looked pretty silly getting into the cold water as gingerly as possible as if doing so would make the sensation less traumatic. We just could not get Dad to go swimming with us. He much more enjoyed watching all the silliness of his daughters and, of course, making films.

The next day we visited Dad's best friend from the Navy, Joe, and his family! They had two boys, and the oldest played the accordion. He was quite talented at it and played several tunes for us. I was very impressed as I had not seen an accordion except on television. We had a very enjoyable visit.

Venturing on a return to Niagara Falls, three years after our first encounter, made the memories more vivid. Besides seeing the fantastic falls again, we visited Louis Tussaud's Waxworks on the

Canadian side. Our parents had a particularly keen interest in taking in the displays of lifelike wax figures of famous people and historical representations. The five of us entered the very glitzy lobby to buy the tickets. Dad could not restrain himself from making a memorable moment for all of us but especially for Terri. In the excitement of the moment, he tapped into her enthusiasm for the idea of seeing people made of wax. He looked down at her and told her to go over to that nice man, all dressed up in the red uniform, standing at the ticket booth and ask him a question. Terri, wanting to please Dad, ran up to the man and tried to get his attention. The more she talked, the more he ignored her. In frustration, she finally reached up and pulled on the tail of his jacket, obtaining no response. It was then that she realized that he was a wax figure. Dad giggled and grabbed her by the hand and escorted us all through the museum's many displays. They were a little too realistic to suit Terri and me. It was a creepy feeling to see them, especially when it came to some of the historically accurate but exceedingly horrifying exhibits. At that point, we little girls were all too happy to leave for merrier adventures.

Our bi-annual trip to Aunt Kay's and Uncle Cal's and family in Trumansburg, New York, was next on the itinerary. They lived in a gorgeous two-story home on a large corner lot. It was white wood framed with a huge enclosed porch in the front and a barn-like garage in the back. A massive, perfectly shaped blue spruce stood in the front yard like a giant sentinel protecting everything around it. It was as tall as the house. Orange tiger lilies lined the driveway on one side.

Roaming through the rooms of Aunt Kay's house was a feast for the eyes. She had a lot of beautiful things. An upright piano with a round stool that rotated sat in a room near the front of the house. I so wanted to play it.

Their little dog brought a lot of curiosity to us. We played with it, and I decided to kiss the dog on the top of the head. My dad had a fit and made me wash my face and hands and forbade me ever to do that again!

Aunt Kay and Uncle Cal had great friends, and they loved to have neighborhood corn roasts. Early in the day, they filled a large shallow hole in the field about four feet across or so with charcoal. When the charcoal burned down to embers, I think they covered them with dirt. They then laid water-soaked corn still in the husks over the soil and put corn stalks on top of the layer of corn to retain the heat for cooking all day. Lots of families showed up to play and eat corn in the evening. It was always a special treat.

On the day we left Aunt Kay's, we played croquet in the front yard with the whole family. I loved doing that and playing chase with my older cousins. After the last memorable moments, with hugs and kisses, we were off to Hazleton, Pennsylvania, to visit with Uncle Harry and Aunt Millie and Aunt Anna, who was newly engaged. A lot of excitement was in the air, and she could not wait to introduce us to her fiancé, John. We were invited to John's house to meet his very kind family. His mother made pierogies and pole beans. Pierogies are small dough dumplings stuffed with a filling such as potato or cheese and are often served with onions and sour cream. They are popular in the countries of Poland, Ukraine, and Russia.

The next morning, Aunt Anna showed us the most beautiful dress I had ever seen up until then. So many fluffy ruffles; yards and yards of them covered that dress. After we talked for a while, Dad, Mom, Kim, and Aunt Anna left, and we spent some quality time with Aunt Millie. She was very kind and enjoyed playing with Terri and me. She taught us how to play *Old Maid* and *Go Fish*, which we really enjoyed!

Aunt Millie talked all day about the pot roast we were going to have for dinner. I was highly anticipating the meal because if it was anything like Mom's pot roast, it would be delicious! When Uncle Harry, Dad, Mom, and Aunt Anna arrived back to the house, the table was set, and we sat down for the feast! It smelled a lot different from Mom's pot roast meals, but I was set for the first bite and could hardly wait. Was I ever in for one of the shocks of my young life! It was definitely not Mom's pot roast; it was a pork roast! I had never heard of such a thing! Now Mom had a rule about eating away from home. Eat at least a little of everything set before you when you are the guest in someone else's home, especially if you are related to them. I tried as best as I could to comply, but secretly, I vowed to myself that I would do my best to keep very far from pork pot roast. The meal's saving grace was mashed potatoes, for which I have always had a great fondness.

We dropped by for hugs, kisses, and farewells the next morning. After taking pictures on the front porch, we headed over to see our Great Aunt Anna, our Granddad's older sister. She lived in a tiny but comfortable and bright apartment in Hazleton. She had a delightful spirit, and before we left, she was invited to come back to St. Louis with us on our return trip! We left her to make her arrangements and went on to Philadelphia.

Grandma Mary had passed away on October 27th, 1961, on the thirty-second anniversary of our Grandma Catherine's passing. Mom told us that she had over 200 descendants. That is a lot of love. She was a precious lady, and the sadness of her passing left Granddad with a loss for words during our visit. Terri and I wrote to him when we returned to St. Louis. He wrote our Mom saying how much he enjoyed the letters from his granddaughters.

Our next big adventure was Atlantic City, New Jersey. With tremendous excitement, Terri and I could hardly contain our anticipation of seeing the Atlantic Ocean again! It was not long before we experienced the salty ocean breezes combing through our hair and the sound of roaring waves. To feel the loose hot, dry sand in contrast to the much harder packed, deceitfully stable wet sand was a very curious sensation. As we made it to the water, Dad peered out across the sea and commented, "Look way, way out there!" As he pointed to the northeast, he tried to convince us that we could see England from our location and acted surprised that we could not make it out! He then filmed our ocean experience, including Kim running out to the water as the tide receded. Kim was dressed in the cutest one-piece black and red plaid bathing suit with a four-inch ruffle at her hipline. She was still a little thing and was so excited to see the big water! She ran toward the outgoing waves as fast as her short legs could carry her, making little splashing sounds all the way! All of a sudden, her eyes got so big! She immediately made a 180-degree turn and ran back, crying, "Daddy, Daddy! Daddy! The waddy's chasing me!"

After that, Dad left us with Mom and headed for the water. I was quite nervous watching him disappear in the enveloping white foam of the waves, but he was almost giddy with each onslaught. It felt great to see the thrill of the moment in his face. Mom was enjoying it also and got some pretty good footage of those brief moments.

We changed and went up to experience the famous Atlantic City Boardwalk. After exploring for a while, Dad found a nice seafood restaurant and took us in. I was about to order tuna when Dad firmly and adamantly reminded us that we could not choose anything that we could eat at home. I do not remember what he ordered for us. As a child, I was not very adventurous concerning food.

Later on, we found a candy shop with a live display of saltwater taffy being made. A humongous blob of chocolate taffy was on this machine in a battle with mechanical arms that stretched and folded and stretched and folded over and over again and would not release the sweet prisoner from its clutches. Eventually, the candyman cut and wrapped the big blob of taffy and sold the pieces to the delighted patrons who could not resist the temptation. The scent of warm sugar and chocolate begged us to follow our noses through the entrance of the old shop, which, by its appearance, had welcomed guests for decades. That was another unique experience. Mom purchased taffy and fudge, and we were off to visit a few more shops and headed back to Philly.

A good night's rest prepared us for a very long trip home. We quickly returned to Hazleton to pick up our very excited Great Aunt Anna. Mom and Dad escorted her to the car and loaded her suitcase into the trunk. Just as she was about to climb into the back seat, she giggled and inquired, "How many days will it take us to get to St. Louis?"

Dad smiled at her, and with a twinkle in his eye, responded, "We will be there tomorrow!"

She was astounded! When she was comfortably in the back seat with Terri and me, we took off. Bless her heart! She then got to partake with us Dad's two primary speeds of travel: flying low and barely stopping. I know she was thrilled when we arrived at the end of an over nine hundred-mile and an at least sixteen-hour trip.

The Year of Fourth Grade

39 - Fourth Grade

ourth grade brought with it two teachers who were married. The wife taught in the morning, and the husband taught in the afternoon. Along with that adjustment came a frightening realization that the principal who had made such a big impression on my life in kindergarten would be my afternoon teacher. I was scared to death!

Mrs. Meyermann taught the morning classes, including Bible, social studies, and reading. Her ability to make social studies come alive gave students a sense of almost being in the locations. One morning she shared Disney's film, *The Living Desert*. That was quite interesting as I had never seen a desert up to that point. Her teaching about Oregon with its high mountains and a seacoast gave me a desire to visit such a beautiful place one day.

The world of social studies was not the only gift that Mrs. Meyermann afforded me. Being very conscious of her students' reading abilities led her to contact my parents concerning my struggle and encourage them to access the library. The whole family went to the St. Louis County Library together for the first time. I was issued my first library card and selected *Heidi* by Johanna Spyri for my first adventure. Reading a book was so different than reading the short stories in our readers, which never made much sense to me. Heidi allowed me to frolic in the mountains with a little shepherd girl and visit her grandfather and friends. I lived out that book in my mind with every page I turned. Heidi had strong relationships with the people around her. Her intentions were often mistaken, and I could relate to that. But the most important thing to me about Heidi was that she had a grandfather! I relished every encounter between them. The next book I read was *Charlotte's Web* by E. B. White. That was a great book about another character who understood sacrifice and was always trying to help others out. I thought that if I knew Charlotte personally, we would be good friends.

Mr. Meyermann, on the other hand, probably had no idea how terrified I was of him. Almost every day, when he came into the room, my heart would sink, and fear would tempt me. One afternoon, I was afflicted with a relentless case of hiccups. Try as I might to suppress every issuance of noise, there was no way they were going to stop on their own. In complete desperation, I gathered up what courage I could and slowly walked to the front of the room and stood beside his desk. With a stammer, I tried as best I could to convey my need for a drink of water. Mr. Meyermann looked into my eyes and said, "If you can hiccup, I will let you go get a drink." He obviously understood that terror would cure hiccups and, of course, terror won. My hiccups were cured, but now I experienced a painful feeling that I believed that my teacher thought I was lying. I went back to my desk in utter shame. I did not know how to convey my misunderstanding to him and therefore lived with that suppressed fear.

Despite my fear, he taught me a lot, and I appreciate that. He had a unique way of curling the papers that he distributed to us, which I will never forget. His technique allowed him to easily count and separate them into the perfect number for each row of students. I had never seen anyone do that before but have mimicked his example for decades since. I especially loved the fact that he taught us how to use graph paper for our math problems. It was an excellent way to keep the columns of figures correctly aligned. He had an appreciation for my ability to excel in math and made sure that I had more advanced books to study. Mr. Meyermann's encouragement in this one subject, built my confidence to a new level.

40 - Junior Girl Scouts and Field Trips

I graduated to the Junior level in Girl Scouts, which lasted through fourth and fifth grade. Our uniforms were green with dark green badge sashes, yellow bow ties, and dark green hats shaped like French berets. Our experiences widened with the addition of more extensive field trips, camping, and educational opportunities.

Field trips were a big thing for all of us. We went to Pevely Dairy and watched them make cottage cheese in enormous vats as big as a room. At a cookie factory, we saw macaroons being mass-produced. Pre-measured squirts of cookie dough were accurately aligned and pressed on to a conveyor belt cookie sheet. They appeared to be soldiers in readiness, awaiting orders to be called into the fiercely heated battle. Enter they did into a massively long oven. Once baked, they were cooled and with great precision re-aligned and loaded into packages and boxed for delivery to the stores. The scent of hot sugary coconut heavy in the air made me want to want to grab some to take home.

We took a tour of Grant's Farm in St. Louis. The Clydesdale horses whose massive size and strength overshadowed the memory of seeing anything else on the trip.

Another outing compelled us to ride the city buses to visit a large grocery store and listen to a meat market manager's presentation. Little did I know that a meat cutter I would meet in Florida in 1974 would become my husband and the love of my life. Had I known then, I might have paid much closer attention. Afterward, we crossed the street for a short visit to a Steak and Shake® for fries and milkshakes. We learned as a group that we could not dawdle, or we would miss the city bus. That led to quite a bit of anxiousness in the girls' hearts who struggled with the pressure of ordering and the speed of which their orders were handled. Several of the girls, including me, had to make a mad dash for the oncoming red and white bus. (On another coincidental note, that future meat cutter of mine gave me my engagement ring at a Steak and Shake.)

Laclede Gas Company held cooking classes, which we attended one summer. The instructor was a very pretty lady. On the first day, we arrived and took our seats in a room with a large table in the front, and a thoroughly modern kitchen staged behind it. We were given little blue folders with all of the recipes we were going to learn to make from "scratch." One of my friends raised her hand and asked where to buy "scratch." The teacher smiled and told us that scratch meant that we would be learning to use separate ingredients and not pre-prepackaged meals from boxes.

We made blushing pear salads, which were half a pear brushed lightly with cherry juice. A little cottage cheese and a cherry were placed in a scooped-out section where the seeds had been. The presentation on lovely lettuce leaves made a very eye-appealing dish. The fact that we used pre-peeled and halved canned pears did not take away from the thrill of creating something pretty and edible.

During another class, we made pickled cheese hot dogs, which consisted of slicing the hot dog longways and placing a strip of cheese and sweet pickles in the groove. They were then heated in the oven and set on hotdog buns for serving.

The third dish we made changed my life and eating habits much to the joy of both my mother and myself. It may not be of consequence to most people, but up to that point, I had only seen hard-boiled eggs, which I loved and gooey lard-ladened fried eggs with rubbery textured edges. The latter convinced me that breakfast was a less than appealing meal at best. The knowledge and ability to scramble light, fluffy eggs gave me a new impression of my most hated meal of the day. It also replaced nightmares of breakfast battles with pleasantly anticipated first meal mornings.

One summer, there was a fascinating field trip for all Girl Scout Troops in the St. Louis area. Samuel Clemens, better known by his pen name, Mark Twain, was the author of two famous books called *The Adventures of Tom Sawyer* (1876) and *The Adventures of Huckleberry Finn* (1884). His boyhood home was in Hannibal, Missouri, and arrangements were made for us to make the trip on a vintage train. It was a hot but beautiful summer day. We boarded the train holding our pre-made lunches of sandwiches, apples, and potato chips packed in white cardboard boxes. Each of us scurried to try to sit by our friends on the antique train seats by the open windows. Soon we heard the clanging bell and the loud whistle as we happily rolled along on our 117-mile trip to the northwest along the Missouri River. We were glad for every breeze that came through the windows, and in a little more than two hours, we pulled in to our destination.

Most all the girls had read Mark Twain's books or had seen the movies made from them. In our minds, we re-lived passages as we viewed the areas around Hannibal that influenced the creation of famous stories of the two orphaned boys and their friends and relatives who lived in the town. We saw the boyhood home of Samuel Clemens, the houses of Becky Thatcher, and Huckleberry Finn, and J. M. Clemens, Justice of the Peace Office. We could imagine what it might have been like to pay Tom for the privilege of whitewashing a fence or listen to the voices of Aunt Polly and Becky Thatcher as they called out to Tom. You could feel the sense of wanting to take off with Huck to go fishing or escape on the river on a raft to board a riverboat or explore the cave that hid Huck's friend, the runaway slave named Jim. Everything in this area of town gave the impression that Mark Twain's characters were genuine and a sense of how they lived. The trip was most impressive, especially made in the company of Girl Scout troop members from all over the St. Louis area[5].

Another summer adventure was a trip to The St. Louis Muny. The Muny, which opened in 1919, is a fantastic outdoor municipal theater with a revolving stage. With great enthusiasm, we attended the live presentation of *The King and I,* featuring Betty White as Anna, the school teacher, and Charles Korvan as the king. It was exciting to see that immense stage revolve for the acts, and the play was marvelous! There is nothing quite like seeing a live stage play, especially as a child. The evening was filled with magnificent music, a sea of colorful costumes, and scenery. As we left the theater, after chatting with friends for a long time and waiting for the crowds to dissipate, we walked down a long breezeway toward the city buses and much to our amazement; we saw Betty White! We did not approach her, but being that close was enough for us. The fact that she had recently married Allen Ludden, the host for the popular television game show, called *Password,* inspired us even more.

41 - Girl Scout Camping Trips

The field trips were one-day experiences, but camping involved weekends and sometimes an entire week. We attended in the summer three camps over the years: Cedarledge, Fiddlecreek, and Ridgetop. There were all sorts of activities. I remember learning to swim at Cedarledge when I was ten. I bought a sailor's hat with the camp name printed on an evergreen emblem. When I grew out of the hat, I cut the stamp off and saved it. (I know when my children read that last statement, they will probably roll their eyes as they cannot believe what I have saved over the years). We also hiked and made crafts. I learned to whittle soap (my bar was carved into an open Bible). Personal name badges were fashioned by whittling off part of the bark on a stick, writing our names on the bare part, and then tying a string to both ends to hang like necklaces. Another craft involved braiding plastic lacing and forming lanyards from which we could hang our pocket knives or whistles. Terri and I made more of these with yellow-orange and white lacing when we returned home.

Being in the fresh air all day substantially increased our appetites making every meal a highly anticipated event. We cooked on homemade stoves called buddy burners that we learned to build. First, we took cleaned out tuna cans and placed a long strip of corrugated cardboard cut to the height of the can and tightly rolled into a coil. Our leaders filled the prepared tuna cans with melted wax called paraffin. Secondly, we took a large juice can and with a little can and bottle opener that had a triangular cutting edge, we cut about five holes at the side of the bottom of the can and then repeated the process at the opposite side near of the top of the can for ventilation. At the campsite, we made a meal by placing a hamburger patty on a piece of aluminum foil. We then put a big slice of raw potato and some canned green beans on top of that. We folded our small meals in aluminum foil. After carefully placing our tuna can burners on a non-burnable surface like a large rock or concrete slab, we lit them and then put the larger can over them. This gave us a cooking surface on which we placed our meals. All of us were pretty hungry by the time our leaders said we could remove the meals from the buddy burners and put them on our camping plates to eat.

Camper's Stew made with fried hamburger meat and onions mixed in with Campbell's Vegetable Soup® was a treat. That was a meal that was often repeated at home when Dad was away. One night we had homemade chili. We made s'mores for dessert after the campfire times made by roasting marshmallows over the campfire and sandwiching them with half of a Hershey's Chocolate Bar® between two graham crackers. Another night we roasted hot dogs on unbent wire coat hangers over the fire.

Campfires glowed after the meal cleanup, and the group hovered around them to giggle, sing songs, do skits and tell stories. There was a television comedy show called The Smother's Brothers. During one of their episodes, they sang a popular parody of the song "On Top of Old Smokey", by Tom Glazer, called "On Top of Spaghetti". It was hysterical!

Not being able to get that song out of my head and with being exposed to parents who loved to make up their own lyrics to songs was all the motivation I needed to create this little ditty and shared it around the campfire:

"On Top of Old Ridgetop"

On top of Old Ridgetop,
All covered with scouts
We lost our poor leaders
In a copperhead's mouth.
We cut open its belly
'Cause we were so sad.
We gave them a funeral
So they wouldn't be mad,
With green and purple flowers.

As the saying goes, I probably should not quit my day job! That was not the only mischief in which I participated. A few of us got the Scout leaders pajamas, soaked them, and froze them in the camp freezer. I cannot believe I did that! It was all in fun, and they took it pretty well.

The camp provided tents that were already installed on wooden floors. Each tent had four army-type cots. Those of us who did not have sleeping bags learned to make our own bedrolls from blankets and sheets.

After the campfire, we broke up, headed down to the restroom to clean up, and then back to the tents. There were four girls in each tent. Crawling into our bedrolls, we reviewed the day's activities and giggled until we heard those unwelcome words, "Go to sleep, girls!" One of my tent mates, who was very tall and thin, was assigned the cot next to the tent opening. The moon was pretty bright one night, and I could see her silhouette in the moonlight. She was lying on her back on the cot and had her knees pulled up, and then she slowly moved one of her long thin arms over the top of her bent knees. My imagination got the best of me, and I thought a snake was attacking her! I was so scared that I could barely breathe, and finally, with one great shrill, I screamed at the top of my lungs, causing an uproar in the camp! Leaders flew out of their tents to run to the source of the chaos. Everyone was shaken up as they were looking for my imaginary snake. Once it was not found, we were all quieted and told to get some sleep. I guess that is what I got for making up that silly song!

The next morning we were met with orange juice, hard-boiled eggs, and "homemade" donuts. These were made from taking canned biscuits and putting a hole in the center and frying them in a cast iron pot of oil over a campfire. Once they were cooked, they were dipped into white sugar and cooled before handing them out. Boy, were they tasty!

We were at camp for a week, which was just long enough to write home and beat the letter there! Camping was an activity we participated in at least once, if not twice a year. Summer camping was pretty enjoyable, but I was not overly fond of fall camping. It could get quite cold, and the camp house we stayed in had an abundance of daddy-long-legs spiders.

42 - Another Physical Change

$\mathcal{M}$om was not content with my appearance. From birth, she never liked my ears because they stuck straight out. Also, the cartilage was very flat, so my ears lacked the lines that most people have. Once she found out that another mother whose son was in my class had solved the same challenge with her son's one ear, my mother was off to the races. She was convinced that people were making fun of me because of my ears and pleaded with Dad to have plastic surgery done to "correct" my "problem."

I remember being made fun of but not because of my ears. I believe that God gave me the ears He wanted me to have with some pretty significant side benefits. Because of the flexibility of my ears, I was able to fold them out over my ear canals to muffle sound when I was trying to sleep. Having overly sensitive hearing, I easily detect mosquitoes flying and ice melting in the night. Mom probably did not realize the benefits I had been given and could only see that my ears stuck out and felt that people would always make fun of them.

Overcoming Dad's resistance, Mom made an appointment. I was about ten when I met the surgeon who took pictures and fashioned a new design to reconstruct my ears to place them closer to my head and put those lines in them. Surgery was scheduled during the summer after fourth grade. My parents took me to the hospital, where the operation and recovery were to take place. I woke up to find my whole head wrapped in so many bandages that I looked like I was wearing a football helmet. The experience reminded me of a terrible *Twilight Zone* episode called "Beauty is in the Eye of the Beholder."

I was required to spend the week at the hospital until they could make sure that the surgery was successful, and I had healed. Dad visited me regularly and brought me flowers that had turned blue because they had been watered with blue food coloring. He was quite compassionate toward me and said he wished that he could take my place. I could see the ache in his heart. I do not remember Mom coming to the hospital to see me at all. Maybe it was hard for her to get someone to watch my sisters.

After a few days in bed, I decided to go exploring. I found a wheelchair, left my room, and headed for the elevator. I went to another floor and did not find anything more exciting than on my floor, so I headed back. When the elevator door opened, the nurse was waiting for me. I got chewed out for leaving the floor! I had no idea it would be a problem!

The girl that shared the room with me had been severely burned in an apartment fire. She was being treated with extremely painful skin grafts to reconstruct her damaged body. If I remember correctly, she had already been there for three months. I felt so bad for the girl who was in such obvious pain. Even so, she had such a beautiful and friendly attitude. A nun visited her one day and brought some divinity candy. I had never had any before, and she asked the nun to give me some of it. It was incredibly sweet!

One nurse seemed to be quite short-tempered with me. She brought in an injection to administer one evening. After wiping the injection site with an alcohol pad, she jabbed me so hard that I grabbed her hand and yanked out the shot. Immediately, she jabbed me again! I am sure she was irritated not only with me but with the stark difference between her two patients: one with life-saving plastic surgery and one with cosmetic surgery.

The day came when my bandages were removed, and I was released. My ears were now flat against my head, smaller than before. I now had plastic inserted under the skin to give the appearance of those curves Mom so desperately desired. The problems that resulted were that I could no longer use my ears to block out sound when necessary, and the plastic gave me greater amplification. I have had slight irritation with the incision scars all of my life. It is no big deal, though. I do not want to seem ungrateful, but looking back, I think that I would have rather been able to sleep better than to have flat immovable ears.

More About Grace

43 - Church

I grew up in the Missouri Synod Lutheran Church. Throughout the year, the story of the life of Jesus Christ and His ministry was the subject of sermons and Sunday School lessons. Each season and celebration had a unique name on the calendar.

The spring ushered in the season of Lent with a deep sense of introspection and the need for salvation. Palm Sunday followed with the celebration of Jesus' triumphant entry into Jerusalem. Maundy Thursday celebrated the remembrance of the first Lord's Supper at the end of the Passover meal. Good Friday mourned His trials and death and made us aware of our need for a Savior. The celebration of Resurrection Sunday reminded believers of the promise of life everlasting to all who trusted in Him as their Savior. Fifty days later, Pentecost celebrated the giving of the Holy Spirit.

Summer lessons were taught from both the Old and New Testaments. The Reformation was remembered in the autumn. It began on October 31st, 1517, when Martin Luther nailed the "95 Theses" to the church door. This act was the spark of the Protestant Reformation. Thanksgiving was celebrated with a church service. There was always a church bazaar around that time of year.

Four weeks before Christmas, Advent celebrated the precious prophecies of the long-awaited Messiah, Jesus, the gift of God. The bustle of noise and excitement was everywhere as plays, music, and decorations were prepared. Many Lutheran churches, Grace included, put up two live Christmas trees, one on each side of the altar. The one on the left of the altar was decorated in all white lights, and the ornaments were crafted in the shapes of Christian symbols. The tree on the right had all colored lights, and a cross made of white lights was attached to the trunk of the tree. To me, the multi- colored lights on that tree reminded me of the Bible verse, "God so loved the world that He gave His only begotten Son, that whosoever believes in Him should not perish but have everlasting life." John 3:16, KJVᴰ.

The Sunday School Children dressed in angel costumes or their Christmas clothes. The children's program was held on the Sunday before Christmas.

The congregational Christmas program included the children's and the adult choirs. Scripture readings and dramatic presentations brought the Christmas story to life. Every song rang out the good news of God's love and the precious gift of His Son, Jesus Christ. The lights in the church were dimmed as more light was directed to those giving the messages. A small group of musicians filled the air with the sounds of violins, cellos, harps and flutes, and several brass instruments. The congregation participated in the singing of hymns. The choirs sang songs about Jesus' birth: "Silent Night," "O Little Town of Bethlehem," and "Away in a Manger." We learned to sing parts and descants, and the children joined in singing some of the songs with the adult choirs and the congregation.

Before the last song, candles were dispersed to everyone. Pastor shared that God, the Father, showed His love in sending Jesus to be the Light of the world. That Light would show us the way to Him. Pastor then lit one candle and used it to light the ushers' candles. They shared their light throughout the congregation until every candle was lit, and the whole church was full of light. This was a picture of how sharing the message of God's love can spread throughout the world. Glowing faces and hearts and voices sang one more beautiful hymn. In closing the heart-stirring service, Pastor shared a blessing telling us now to take the Light of Jesus Christ out into the world and share this love. This is the true meaning of Christmas!

One moment between my dad and me happened on a Christmas morning after the service. Almost everyone had left the sanctuary. We returned hymnals and Bibles to the book racks attached to the back of the pews. Gathering things left behind, he paused and looked at me with such tender eyes. In an unusually gentle tone, he asked, "Jilene, what is the name of the song we sang this morning about the rose?" I could feel that the words truly touched his heart and responded with, "Lo, How a Rose E'er Blooming!" He told me that it was one of his favorite hymns.

"Lo, How a Rose E'er Blooming"*

1 Lo, how a rose e'er blooming
From tender stem hath sprung!
Of Jesse's lineage coming
As prophets long have sung,
It came a flow 'rlet bright,
Amid the cold of winter,
When half-spent was the night.

2 Isaiah 'twas foretold it,
The rose I have in mind;
With Mary we behold it,
The virgin mother kind.
To show God's love aright,
She bore to us a Savior,
When half-spent was the night.

3 This flow 'r, whose fragrance tender
With sweetness fills the air,
Dispels with glorious splendor

The darkness ev'rywhere.
True man, yet very God,
From sin and death he saves us
And lightens ev'ry load.

4 O Savior, child of Mary,
Who felt our human woe;
O Savior, King of glory,
Who dost our weakness know:
Bring us at length we pray
To the bright courts of heaven,
And to the endless day[6].

A week later, services were held on New Year's Eve. What a beautiful way to end the current year, remembering what the Lord had done in our lives and asking His blessings and guidance for the New Year!

44 - Our Pastor

Our minister at Grace Lutheran Church was Reverend Kurt Biel. He never liked to be called Reverend and always wanted to be called Pastor Biel. He easily kept my attention as he spoke of God and Jesus and the Holy Spirit. At a young age, I pondered the things that he related in the messages. After service, he always had the congregation stand to bless us from Numbers 6:24-26 KJVᴱ. (This is known as the "Aaronic Blessing.") Making the sign of the cross in front toward us, he would say:

"May the Lord bless thee and keep thee,
May the Lord make his face shine upon thee, and be gracious unto thee,
May the Lord lift up His countenance upon thee,
And give thee peace!"

Even now, the memory of this special blessing and the love of God that was heard in Pastor Biel's comforting voice puts tears in my eyes. I feel as if God Himself reaches out to me with a heart-warming embrace every time I hear it.

After this benediction, Pastor Biel walked down the middle aisle and stood at the double doors at the back of the church to talk to each church member as they exited. During one Sunday, I was especially touched by the message, and when it was my turn to greet him, he reached down to shake my hand. I said to him, "Pastor, you are a good Pastor!" He looked at me and told me, "No, I am not a good Pastor." He then took the moment to help me understand that any good that I saw in him only came from God! I did not know the word humble yet, but I experienced it in talking with this kind pastor with compassionate eyes. I thank God that He uses the hearts of humans to express so great a love.

On another Sunday, a few years later, we sat listening to Pastor Biel when he remarked, "The Greek for this word is..." That caught my attention, and I raised my hand to ask how he knew that?! In the Lutheran church, you do not raise your hand and ask questions during a service. By the time we were dismissed, I forgot to ask him about his statement, but it stayed in the back of my mind. When I was about thirty-five years old, the seed which was planted in my mind when I was about eight years old started to sprout. I was told that the Bible was originally written in Hebrew and Chaldean for the Old Testament and Greek for the New Testament! I was also introduced to a *Strong's Exhaustive Concordance* (a book that lists all the words used in the King James Bible with the corresponding original Hebrew or Greek words, the meanings and the references where they are used in the text. It is available for the English Stand Version© and New American Standard Version© also).

Pastor Biel and his family continued to touch our lives from the time of my birth until I was twelve, and we left St. Louis. His influence did not stop then as we found him again when we moved to Orlando, Florida, four years later. His genuine and dedicated pastoral care would impact our family for decades: from conversion, counseling, Christenings, confirmations, marriages, and comfort. The very last time I saw him, he had long since retired but made a precious appearance at my dad's funeral in 1993 — what a wonderful blessing God gave to us in this faithful pastor.

45 - Church Activities and Picnics

$\mathcal{G}$race Lutheran Church was at the center of our lives, and much of our activities stemmed from there. There were Sunday School classes, adult classes, and confirmation classes for membership. There were men's groups, ladies' groups like the Dorcas Society, the Women's Missionary League, and the quilting group. Children's activities included Boy Scouts, Girl Scouts, and Vacation Bible School. Pancake suppers were held by the men, and spaghetti suppers were put on by the women.

The Fall Bazaars brought opportunities for the community to purchase homemade crafts and baked goods. Many useful items like aprons, quilts, crocheted hankies (Mom made quite a number of those) other crocheted or knitted items, and plenty of decorations lined the tables. It was great fun to see the displays and try to persuade Mom to purchase some of the offerings.

In the spring, talent shows brought out many otherwise unseen performances of hidden actors and actresses, singers, and musicians, much to the delight of their audiences. Bake sales beckoned the sweet-toothed among the congregants. Cake-walks filled the atmosphere with laughter and cheers as person after person was left standing and empty-handed of the delectable prize they sought in the contest of musical chairs. The year that Red Velvet Cake hit the church circuit, I think every woman there tried her hand at it. Of course, Mom's contribution to those confectionery fundraisers was her delectable carrot cake.

One of the activities at Grace that I enjoyed the most was Vacation Bible School. For two weeks during the summer, children came in the mornings to have Chapel, Bible lessons, crafts, playground time in the park next door, and refreshments of cookies and Kool-aid®. Each year had a different Bible theme from which all the activities were centered. I still have my favorite craft, a picture of Jesus praying in Gethsemane, leaning over a large rock. It was a carving etched into a piece of heavy green foil and attached to a piece of cardboard and framed with pieces of wood. I love the reminder of His love and sacrifice for me and all who love Him. At the end of the two weeks was a celebration.

I did have a bit of a trial one year in the park next to the church. I was climbing the ladder of the big slide. When I grabbed the curved rail at the very top, I was stung by a wasp that did not appreciate the caress! All I could do was scream until the person behind me convinced me to go down the slide. I remember that at least two of the classmates walked me back to the church and helped me find the assistant pastor, Pastor Bohlman. He removed the stinger from my thumb, releasing me from that awful sharp burning pain. He was so kind and had beautiful white hair. I was very grateful that he was there to help me.

Another time I was on the merry-go-round, which was going faster than I could handle. The ones who were pushing it would not relent and let me off. Trying to disembark at neck-breaking speed was not the wisest thing I ever tried to do. I determined to jump, and instead of landing on my feet, I slid across the pavement on my face. Not too smart!

The other exciting church event for the summer was the picnic held on the grounds. Nearly everyone showed up for it. Each group in the church had some activity or booth in which they participated to try to raise funds. Tickets were sold for all the typical booths that lined the parking lot.

The dunking machine enticed members to throw baseballs at a target, which caused a victim, sitting on a plank, to fall into a tub of water. That person had the privilege of heckling the people that tried to get him soaked. Lots of laughter surrounded that booth. The Girl Scouts ran the fishing booth for the children who offered up their tickets for small prizes like kazoos and yo-yos and other trinkets. The Boy Scouts also had special activities. The men cooked hot dogs and hamburgers. The women took care of the bake and craft sales.

An area was set up on the south side of the church under the carport where the craft items and baked goods were sold. I thoroughly enjoyed perusing the tables showing off all those beautiful items. Blankets and quilts and all kinds of crocheted items, including cross-shaped bookmarks and handkerchiefs trimmed in delicately crocheted edges, were displayed ever so carefully. Doll and baby clothes were often set out to entice buyers.

One year, there were two little white china wall plaques in the shape of opened books with prayers painted in gold on the pages. They both had a child kneeling on the ledge in front of the book as if they were saying the prayers. One child had pink pajamas, and the other had blue pajamas. Of course, I wanted to have the one in pink, but when Mom bought them, she gave me the blue one. I was a little disappointed, but over the years, the little prayer on my plaque encouraged me to be the person I have become.

> "Help us to do the things we should,
> To be to others kind and good.
> In all we do and in all we say,
> To grow more loving every day!"

It was at the church picnic that Mom bought those two devotional books, *Little Visits With God* and *More Little Visits with God*. I loved reading those one-page stories. She also purchased our little Lutheran prayer books.

A display of hobby contest entries lined the tables in a large meeting room in the basement. I received third place when I was nine, for my doll clothes I made by hand. The outfit included a gathered yellow skirt, a white top with tiny yellow and orange flowers and green leaves, a yellow vest, and a reversible French hat with a hole for her ponytail. The doll I made the clothes for was a Debbie the Elegant Doll®, like the popular Barbie® doll. I was so excited! I could not believe that I won a ribbon as the competition in the contest included all ages!

At the end of the picnic, drawings for prizes were held. I vaguely remember music being played and an area set up to watch the entertainment. We all had great fun and usually stayed until after cleanup. Then we all collapsed in the car and headed home.

Southside, Northside, All About Downtown Wellston

46 – The Southside of Easton Avenue

The only times I remember shopping in Wellston with Dad was at Central Hardware on the corner of Easton Avenue and Kienlen Avenue. We parked in the lot behind the store. Terri and I hopped out and raced to grab his hands. Walking with Dad on the sidewalks seemed like being in a race. He was always in a big hurry, and we took three steps for every one of his great big steps. The vision of flying low over the weathered concrete sidewalk holding Dad's hand is forever etched in my memory.

Within moments we were inside on a well-calculated mission akin to a military operation. The focus was to advance, conquer, retrieve, and retreat. The purchase was pre-determined, and we were unwaveringly ushered to the specific aisle for the conquest. Any attempt to divert the goal by browsing along the way was met with the orders,"look with your eyes, not with your hands." This tactic ensured that little time would be wasted because the purchase was usually the result of a job requiring immediate attention. Thus, little opportunity availed itself for becoming too intimately familiar with the merchandise displayed. Although very curious about our surroundings, we girls were more than content because of the personal time spent with Dad.

On the other hand, Mom loved to shop! Her method was more like a lengthy military campaign, determined to leave no stone unturned. It was not so much the shopping as it was the hunt for items that she wanted. On top of this, she was beyond thrifty. The term "penny pincher" was secretly worn by her as a badge of honor. I often remarked as an adult that "Mom would not buy anything until Lincoln screamed." Usually, we went to the stores "just to look." If she really liked something, we stalked it every week until it went on sale. The first sale was never good enough, and we returned every week thereafter until she deemed the price worth spending. I believe her thriftiness was deeply seeded in her difficult childhood.

One of her favorite things to do was to get us dressed and head for downtown Wellston. We walked several blocks, made a right turn, and went into a little corner grocery to buy her favorite cola, candy necklaces, and tiny wax bottles filled with fruit-flavored liquid. The thought of wearing candy around our necks seemed pretty exciting back then but now seems pretty disgusting.

After those purchases, we headed past Wellston High School. I was often struck by the architecture of the stately building constructed in 1940. I loved the appearance of the majestic looking stairways and columns. It seemed like a fascinating place, and I was intrigued as to what went on inside. I never got the chance to find out since the school was closed in 1962 before I was old enough to attend.

Around the corner past the school, we turned left heading toward Easton Avenue, the main street of downtown Wellston. We passed Central Hardware on the corner, Wellston Movie Theatre, and on to the stores of the day's focus.

It seemed that we spent many hours in each store. One of my earliest memories was of Mom being so busy on her hunt looking through fabric that I started looking for something to do. I lost track of her, and then I noticed her coat going out the door without me! I thought she had forgotten me, so I raced out onto the sidewalk, and about three stores down the road, I caught up with her. I hurriedly reached for her hand, and this lady turned around and looked at me in such surprise! "YOU'RE NOT MY MOMMY!!" I gasped in bewilderment! I backed away from the surprised lady wearing my mother's coat and rushed back into the store, crying. I found Mom and could not believe that she was wearing the exact same coat as the lady! My heart was pounding, but once Mom understood my confusion, she had no problem convincing me to keep closer to her while she was making her selections.

The jewelry shop where Mom bought a small sterling silver cross for my birthday present one year stood next. It was kind of odd to me that she purchased a beautiful silver ring with an amethyst for another birthday. I was somewhat disappointed as I had hoped for my birthstone. Mom's habit of buying items to grow into also accompanied this purchase. To help with the size dilemma, she also purchased a ring guard. Unfortunately, it was uncomfortable and did not work well. I wore the ring to school, and during gym class, the teacher had us run the entire circumference of the ballpark next to the school. I rounded the second of the three diamonds. While swinging my arms, the ring flew off of my hand and landed in the grass, never to be found again.

A department store was our next destination. It had a toy and crafts department. I was fascinated by the baby-doll bottles with disappearing milk and juice. We bought several craft items there and also my green scrapbook and autograph books. Further down the road was a Walgreens drug store. Mom got her makeup and magazines and took her photograph film there to have it processed. A week later, her prints were ready for pick up.

Leaving Walgreens®, we crossed the trolley tracks to go to the Kresge® five and dime store. Over our years in Wellston, it changed owners and became a Jupiter® store. Five and dimes carried necessities that usually began at the price of a nickel or dime and went upwards of several dollars. They were chain stores that sold all sorts of goods, including clothes, toys, records, puzzles, paint sets, housewares, and school supplies. We bought our Big Chief® tablets, crayons, coloring books, pencils, Nifty® notebooks, notebook paper and big pink erasers there.

Kresge® had a soda fountain counter with bar stools in the front of the store. They sold breakfast and lunch items such as hotdogs, hamburgers, and sandwiches. Sometimes Mom treated us with a special snack. She had lemon added to her cola, Terri ordered hers with cherry syrup, and I got mine with chocolate syrup. We each ordered hotdogs with whatever toppings we wanted. I was always partial to a thin stripe of mustard and sweet relish.

On most of our expeditions, we crossed the street to visit more stores on Easton Avenue's south side. A National Shirt Shop® displayed the latest in men's dress shirts. It had a big window, and the shirts were neatly folded and sported fashionable ties of every color. We often went into a dress shop called Three Sisters® that carried ladies' and girls' clothing. This is where Mom purchased many of our special occasion clothes.

Another five and dime store named Woolworth was next to the dress shop. It was much like Kresge but had brighter lighting and a larger eating area. It seems I always had either egg-salad sandwiches or tuna-salad sandwiches there. They used sweet pickle relish in their salad sandwiches where Mom preferred making hers with dill pickle relish.

Our next destination was JCPenney®. We spent more time there than in any other store in town. The sparkling walkway of the large covered entry welcomed shoppers through storefront windows angled in an offset modern appearance. It was three stories with a "bargain basement." One of Mom's major purchases was her speckled pastel melamine dishware set. They came in various complementary colors: robin's egg blue, and pale shades of pink, yellow, and green. The dishes and serving pieces were displayed right inside the front door, hailing her attention. I cannot even imagine how many times we walked around the display as she anticipated them being marked down at a later date! Over what seemed like a year, Mom bought one or two pieces at a time until her set was complete. She was so proud of those dishes!

Once we got past the dishes, there was a great variety of clothing and household items displayed. Men's clothing was on the first floor. Many a tie and tie tack were purchased by us for Dad. Ladies' and children's clothing were up the stairs to the right. At the top of the staircase was a book display for children. We girls would stare lovingly at the racks. On two particular visits, we were on the second floor long enough to finish reading *Sleeping Beauty* and *The Princess and the Pea*. (I secretly have wondered over the years if I was really not the princess as I have always struggled with sleep.)

Like most every child who has tried at least once, we also found a few moments to play hide and seek and race through the rows of clothing display racks. Boy, were we in trouble when we were caught!

The bargain-basement was a delight as I got a little older and became interested in sewing. A fabric and sewing machine department was located there. We spent hours picking out patterns and fabric for Mom to make clothes for us. The first pattern I bought came from JCPenney®.

The last store we visited on the south side of Easton Avenue was smaller than the five and dimes. It carried similar items, with the addition of books, record albums, paint by number sets and toys. We bought several of each of those which provided hours upon hours of entertainment.

47 – The Northside of Easton Avenue

The north side of Easton Avenue was home to the Victory Theater. We saw Disney's *Bambi*, the cartoon story about a deer, and his life growing up in a forest. Bambi had a best friend who was a rabbit named Thumper. Parts of it were very scary. We also saw *Pollyanna*, the story of a young orphaned girl. She turned the hearts of those around her upside-down.

Heading west from the theater were several other shops. Mom frequented a large dress store named Emporium. It had the typical huge window displays with all the latest fashions. A separate self-standing glass display was built outside the entrance to the store. Customers walked around it to admire the contents in a full 360-degree view. Inside, a grand staircase led to the ladies' department. The dressing rooms stood in two parallel rows. The doors to each stall remained open when not in use. Full-length mirrors hung diametrically opposed to their twins across the hallway. My sisters and I loved to go in and stand in the walkway to see our reflection multiply infinitely. A three-way mirror at one end of the room expanded the mystery even further and totally perplexed us.

Salle Ann, another clothing store, was on the corner of Easton Avenue and Hodiamont Avenue. A five- or six-story office building stood behind it. Its proximity across from the bus and trolley station made it an excellent location for medical and law offices. We entered the building and went to the elevator, manned by a uniformed elevator operator, waiting to transport people to their desired floors. He was the first friendly face met inside the building, and a safety guard for all who entered. The elevator had two sets of doors. The outer set was solid metal, but the inner set was composed of highly polished bronze-colored crisscrossed bars that collapsed on themselves when opened. For any young mind observing their mechanics, they were a temptation to operate. Therefore, the elevator attendant was a welcome sight, especially to parents needing to escort their children to the doctor's offices on the upper floors. After determining our destination, he safely delivered us to the floor where our doctors were located.

Dr. Ira Davis was the doctor who delivered all three of us girls. He was very tall and friendly. His name was painted on his office door. The walls in the hallway were half glass and half wood. The lobby was spacious, had green walls and dark leather and wood furniture. When called, we entered the rather large examining and treatment room, brightly illuminated by the sunlight filtering through the opened windows. I do not recall ever seeing a nurse or receptionist. If I remember correctly, Dr. Davis was a widower and had lost his only child. He was very kind, compassionate with smiling eyes. I really liked him, but I was terrified of shots! I would stall and hope he would not notice me. Terri, on the other hand, seemed to have no fear and, in fact, was very interested in what Dr. Davis was doing. He gave her a shot one time, and she got her face so close to her arm that he remarked that if he was not careful, she would get the needle stuck on her nose! I was, unfortunately, quite the opposite. It took both Mom and Dr. Davis to hold me down to give me a shot. I tensed up so much that I wound up getting a charley horse in my leg and could barely walk.

A chiropractor was in the same building. When I was in first grade, I was jumping rope at recess and collapsed on the playground in severe pain. It turned out that one of my legs was growing much faster than the other, and with adjustments from the chiropractor for about six weeks, I was much better. A side benefit for my mom was that I learned to give relaxing neck and shoulder massages.

A little shop on the first floor of the building sold ladies' and men's hats. Hats were in fashion in the 1950s. Dad and Mom both wore them, and Mom wore gloves when she was dressed up to go out for a special occasion. She called the store a haberdashery.

The Loop Building was located across the street and anchored Easton Avenue's northwest corner and Hodiamont Avenue. Built in 1928, it had initially been Nugents & Bros. Dry Goods Company®. During my childhood, Katz Drug Company® was located on the first floor, and the upper floors held offices.

The Wellston Loop was a main connection boarding area for trolleys and city buses. Wellston, at the time, was quite a bustling area. The man for whom Wellston was named was Erastus Wells, known as St. Louis' father of public transportation. He was the first to bring the trolleys, also known as streetcars, west of the Mississippi River in 1849. I remember riding one that left us off on Page Boulevard west of Hodiamont Avenue. They were powered by overhead electrical wires. It was a lot of fun hearing the clanging as it stopped and started to load or unload passengers. The buses were added to the transportation and extended destinations beyond the range of the streetcar lines. When we could ride the bus that stopped in front of our house, we started using their services instead. The buses replaced the streetcars in the St. Louis area with the last run of the Hodiamont Streetcar Line ending at midnight on May 21st, 1966.

Often, when Dad was out of town, we might stop by the tiny White Mill diner, which was a quick burger place at the Wellston Loop. It was so small that while patrons waited, they could watch the grill cook make their orders. Outside, passengers waiting for buses or streetcars dodged hundreds of pigeons that picked at scraps of bread and other discarded items.

When our bus arrived at the loop, we climbed aboard, and Mom let us drop the coins for the fare into the collection machine mounted next to the bus driver. He had a coin sorter attached to a belt to his side for making change for the passengers. As the coins dropped into the machine, they were sorted and disappeared through a small trap door mechanism. Funny noises were heard from the coins rolling around in the machine as we found our seats on the bus. If we left at the right time, we listened to the bells of a little church on Hodiamont Avenue as we passed. It always put an enthusiastic smile on my face, and I felt like I was getting a little hug from God, which made the trip even more enjoyable. Turning the corner we headed west on Page Boulevard. We anticipated pulling the cord on the wall of the bus to notify the driver of our desire to disembark. Mom carefully taught us to do that when we were just shy of a block from our house. We did not live far from the station, but the bus ride home was very welcomed after a long day in downtown Wellston.

Sometimes, we walked home instead, continuing west on Easton Avenue past Wellston State Bank. Further along the street, a store displayed glass and ceramic items which Mom enjoyed perusing as she was an avid collector of salt and pepper shakers. Also, in those days, many girls collected little glass dolls for their birthdays. Each figurine had a number conspicuously built into the design, and their sizes increased with the ages they were portraying. They wore antebellum dresses and were quite delightful. I wanted them when I was growing up, but I guess Mom did not feel they were practical, or maybe we just did not really have room to display them. It's okay, the memory of pressing my nose up to the glass case is enough. I did buy Mom a set of three small buffalo figurines for Mother's Day. They were pretty cute, especially the calf.

We visited the shoe store at least twice a year. I remember getting saddle oxfords, black patent leather dress shoes, penny loafers, and Keds® tennis shoes over the years. Mom always bought our shoes a size bigger than we needed. It was a challenge because I always wore the shoes out before my feet were big enough to wear them!

Occasionally, we ate at a tiny diner close to the shoe store. One night, I was looking at the menu, and they had soup. Mom led me to try the beef barley soup. I did not know what that was, but I always loved the taste of beef and ordered it. It turned out to become one of my very favorite soups.

We spent an incredible amount of time in downtown Wellston. The noises, the hustle-bustle, sights, scents, tastes, and feelings linger strongly in my memory.

48 - The State Bank of Wellston

The State Bank of Wellston was located at the corner of Easton Avenue and Kienlen Avenue[7,8]. It had an immense cone-shaped tower sign erected high into the air, looking much like something from the space age. A grand cylinder-shaped metal structure surrounded the pinnacle and individually displayed each letter of the bank's name. The building itself was a beautifully designed modern architectural structure. Its facade was enveloped in highly polished granite walls arranged in five parallel but offset angles. The entry was also set at an angle behind wall-sized windows. A scale for the weight conscious conspicuously called from the corner of the entrance hall to the right of the doors. It cost a penny to use. Most people did not own personal scales at the time. Mom was very slender in those days and would sometimes invest a penny for vanity's sake. Inside the second set of glass doors was a large, well furnished lobby.

Dad and Mom helped us set up our first Christmas savings account. We deposited twenty-five cents every other week until we reached five dollars, and that was the money we saved to buy presents for one another. The people at the bank were outgoing and encouraging. We were always given a safety lollipop after making our investments. From the teller stations, we could see the open bank vault with its iconic round door. It made us feel that our money was well protected.

About two weeks after Thanksgiving, Mom took us to the bank to withdraw our Christmas savings accounts. Proudly carrying our little savings accounts booklets, we approached the teller, and each requested the balance of our funds. This moment in time came with mixed feelings. After saving all year, we closed the accounts, but the thoughts of delighting each other on Christmas day with the gifts we acquired added to the joy.

The tellers gave us the annual Christmas Carols booklet. They had ten Christian Christmas songs complete with the written music, and the authors' name. This was so exciting! I cherished these little books. I am sure that they were given with the intent that people would share the experience of caroling in the streets or singing with each other in their homes over the Christmas holidays.

We left the bank with cash and lollipops in hand and headed for the adventure of finding Christmas gifts. On our way toward JCPenney®, we stopped by Three Sisters®. Mom was looking through the clothes and Terri, and I headed for the jewelry counter. We spied a crystal bead necklace with a matching pair of clip-on earrings. Neither one of us could make the purchase ourselves, so we pooled our funds. With great delight, we completed the transaction for Mom's Christmas present. We were so thrilled! Next, we made it to the big glass window at JCPenney®. I had made up my mind that the perfect gift for Dad was a tie tack with his initial. Dad wore ties, and seeing him dressed up made me feel so proud. He had an excellent taste in ties.

The purchases of the gifts for Mom and Dad left Terri and me with a dollar apiece. We searched and searched for just the right gift for our baby sister, Kim. When we finally headed back to the bus loop to go home, Mom decided to stop by Walgreens® drug store. There it was! It was perfect for Kim! We pooled our last two dollars together and bought the cutest brown teddy bear for her! She loved it, and next to her Mrs. Beasley® doll, it became her most treasured possession!

That Christmas shopping day in Wellston is one of my most cherished memories. The excitement that Terri and I shared together and the willingness to combine our funds to get those gifts was great for us both!

On a side note, Dad came home from going to the bank one afternoon carrying three boxes, one for each of us girls. A special promotion from the bank brought a chance to get some cast metal banks in the shape of old cars. They were bronze in color and heavy. They also had a locking door on the bottom. It surely made it easier to save our money to take to the bank in the years to come, a major improvement to the glass piggy banks we had previously used. There were only two ways to get the money out of them. One method was to take a butter knife and coerce the resistant coins or dollar bills to slide down the blade through the slotted opening. If all else failed, and times were desperate, you could just smash the bank. The first method was much more desired both for teaching patience and safety! My little car bank sits on my shelf to this day.

The first week of the next year brought with it another trip to The State Bank of Wellston. Bearing our first twenty-five cents, we opened the following Christmas Club Savings account. We wondered what the end of the year would bring.

Feeling More Grown-up

49 - Fifth Grade

ifth grade seemed to be a mile marker for many reasons. Our classroom started in one location and then was moved to the wing, which housed the mysterious upper-level grades. Somehow this gave students the idea that they were much more grown up and responsible. This feeling was enhanced with changing classrooms for some of our subjects. Also, the upper levels had little interaction with the younger students. We had "arrived" so to speak.

Mr. McWhirter was the teacher who taught the majority of our classes. Every day started with lessons about God and faith. We began to dig a little more into our Bibles and hymnals, which I dearly loved.

Our morning lessons followed with English, math, science, and history. He also noticed my enjoyment in mathematics and thought that I would like to tutor a fellow student during recess. I was so excited, but when I told Dad, he did not share my feelings and informed Mr. McWhirter that I needed to have recess. I was so disappointed, but that was okay, Dad was right.

After recess and lunch, we returned to class for art lessons. Pencil-drawing lessons familiarized us with shapes, shading, dimensions, and distance relationships. Mr. McWhirter painstakingly walked us through these concepts, which made us more observant of the world around us. His lessons on creating images of nearly perfect trees with balanced limbs helped our renderings become worthy of a landscape architect's attention. It was easy to tuck those pictures in my art folder and proudly share them with my parents.

Mr. McWhirter also was very determined to share a specific object lesson about keeping the classroom neat and clean. He waited all week to see how we would respond, and on Friday, he shared the results of his experiment. After reiterating the lesson, he got up from his desk, walked to the back corner of the room, and picked up a crumpled five-dollar bill. It had been laid on the floor the week before. He returned to the front of the class and displayed the ignored prize. Had anyone noticed and returned it, the cash would have been the reward for conscientiousness. You can imagine the groans from his students as they realized that they had just lost a valuable opportunity. Lesson well taken.

Physical education and health followed art. In my great apprehension, I was finally under the instruction of the eighth-grade teacher. You remember, the one who accompanied the principal, Mr. Meyermann, to find me on the bus on the day of the "writing my name on the back of the seat on the bus" escapade. My fear of Mr. Hingst was equal to my fear of Mr. Meyermann. So needless to say, my heart had a hard time hiding my feelings. Accompanied by my queasiness with all things medical and my less than enthusiastic feelings about running, the thought of being taught by Mr. Hingst was, for me, a foreboding situation. One of the things I see looking back is a missed opportunity to transform my fear into a motivation to run faster. It is sad how a past situation can so discolor any positive impression for future encounters. I heard later on in life that the students who sat under Mr. Hingst considered him an excellent eighth-grade teacher. Alas, I had to take their word for it as I did not get that opportunity.

Music and handwriting were subjects taught by the seventh-grade teacher, Mr. Toensing, an exceptional educator. I can still envision him carefully withdrawing a recording of classical music from its paper sleeve and placing it ever so gently on a record player. He asked us to close our eyes and imagine what the music was about. The sound of "The Flight of the Bumble Bee" and "William Tell's Overture" still linger in my mind. He taught us the basics of reading music and made the assignment to write our own song (however humble the creation was). It was fascinating to see the score and the different notes, both in shape and meaning. I began to see music as a language with all its complexities of order, creativity, and emotion.

Mr. Toensing had a quote inscribed on a plaque and placed it under the clock in the back of the room. It was there for those of us who had a challenge keeping our minds on our studies. It subtly imparted the message, "Time Will Pass, Will You?"

Fifth grade was a time for growing and stretching. It was also a time for greater awareness of the everyday cares of the world around us. On Friday afternoon, November 22, 1963, the whole school was summoned to the cafeteria. Students in every classroom glanced at each other in curiosity and a sense of foreboding. A cloud of severe sadness attended the call to gather. Upon reaching our spots in quiet whispers, the student body focused their eyes on Mr. Meyermann. He desired to convey the message to us at school, where consolation was available. I am sure that there was great concern that none of us were alone when we heard. With sadness and compassion, he shared the news that shook our nation that day. Our President, John F. Kennedy, had died. The news stunned us all. Hearts were broken, cries were heard, and streams of tears flooded the eyes of so many. Details were not shared at that time and were not needed as we could barely grasp the shock we now faced.

Dismissed to our classrooms, we prepared to leave for the day. Whimpers of grieving children and whispers of teachers painfully filtered through the hallways. We cleared our desks and waited for the bell to release us. We had a beautiful blessing in sharing the closing of each day with prayer. At that moment, even breathing was hard. It was my turn to pray. Mr. McWhirter called me to the front of the room. Almost blinded by tears welling up from my soul, I made my way to his desk. An ache like a stone in my throat choked me. In excruciating pain, the words, "Dear God," managed to cross my lips before the flood of tears broke from my heart. Mr. McWhirter gently consoled me and continued the words that I could not find to utter. The grief of the nation affected almost everything from that point on. Everyone grew much older and more fearful. The steadying attitude and comforting words of our teachers, families, and friends helped us get through the months that followed. I thank God for those who can step outside their own grief to help others around them.

Two side notes are worth mentioning here:

I connected with Mr. Toensing many years later in 2001 and told him how much he and the valuable lessons he taught had meant to me. He chuckled when I reminded him about the clock!

I finally located Mr. McWhirter in the early 2000s. We had both left Concord in the fall of 1965. He became a school superintendent in Colorado. Eventually, he went into the ministry and was in Tennessee when I caught up with him again. In our conversation, we shared our lifetime experiences, and I thanked him for his instrumental influence, which continued throughout my life.

50 - Memories
Made in the Cafeteria

*I*n schools all over, cafeterias were and still are multi-purpose assembly areas. No recollection of school lunchrooms would be complete without mentioning the most memorable foods. The lunchroom ladies always greeted us cheerfully. Everything in those days was made from scratch. Pizza was a welcome meal with its thick crust, sweet tomato sauce, and a healthy helping of mozzarella cheese. Excellent! My absolute favorite meal was the most fantastic beef stew, which my taste buds embraced! The ingredients were beef, potatoes, carrots, and celery. It was as if the entire combination had been pressure cooked or steamed. The texture was incredibly tender. A thick piece of sweet cornbread with butter and syrup complemented the main dish. A tasty yellow cake with milk chocolate icing completed the meal. Whole white milk was always served with every lunch.

I look back with fondness to the days of the individual milk bottles. Made of thick glass, they held a half-pint. Their tops were doubly sealed with a tabbed white cardboard insert and a larger circle of waxed cardboard was crimped over the bottle's opening protecting the drinking edge. In the afternoon, the younger grades received an extra serving of milk in their classrooms. On Tuesdays and

Thursdays, they were allowed to choose chocolate milk with the permission of parents. Children seemed to get a second wind when they heard the cart rattle down the halls to their rooms.

After lunch, the cafeteria became a gymnasium, mostly when the weather was inclement. Group exercise, basketball, and volleyball were substituted for outside activities. My favorite move in basketball was pivoting. I was not much in favor of indoor sports and preferred softball on the field as it was less of a contact sport.

The cafeteria became an auditorium for general assemblies, band classes, and science exhibitions. One of my science projects displayed was a homemade flashlight that Dad taught me to make. It was a battery, and a flashlight bulb taped on opposite ends of a wooden ruler. He showed me how to attach a wire to make a complete current to work the light. That was fun for me.

Occasionally, the whole school was called to the cafeteria for select Cardinal baseball games. This was also the case when they won the World Series in 1964.

The transformation of the cafeteria into a theater for school plays was the crown event. I was chosen to sing part of the song, *The Old Chisholm Trail*. We practiced many times in the cafeteria, and finally, the performance night arrived. With great anticipation, I longed for my dad to be in the audience, but he was out of town. Mom was out there, and I saw her. It was my turn to step out and sing with all the gusto I could manage, I belted out the following words,

"Now come along boys and listen to my tale
And I'll tell you all my troubles on the old Chisholm Trail!"

Chorus:

"Come-a ti yi yippy, yippy, yay, yippy yay!
Come-a ti yi yippy, yippy, yay!

With my seat on the saddle and my hat in the sky
I'll quit punchin' cows in the sweet by and by!"

Repeat chorus.

Little did I know that Dad entered the front doors of the school just in time to hear his daughter clearly sing out her cowboy song. From the stage, I saw him, grinning from ear to ear, and his chest bursting with pride! He made it! He made it! I could not believe my eyes. On that day, he proved he was my biggest fan!

51 - Girl Scouts - Juniors to Cadettes

uesdays, after school, were like an island for developing friendships and experiencing the world outside of our regular activities. In Junior Girl Scouts, we began working on badges, and this learning activity continued through the Cadette level. Some were achieved simultaneously with the rest of the troop members. I especially enjoyed choosing the ones I wanted to earn. Before finishing my Girl Scouting career, twenty-one badges from the Junior level and three from the Cadette level hung neatly arranged and sewn on my badge sash.

The names of the badges were:

<u>Junior Level</u>

Toymaker
Troop Camper
Housekeeper
Backyard Fun
Hospitality
Cook
Personal Health
My Home

Needlecraft
Health Aid
Collector
Dabbler
Gypsy
Water Fun
Active Citizen
Drawing and Painting
Troop Dramatics
Home Health and Safety
My Trefoil
Community Safety
My Troop

The next level of Girl Scouts I participated in was Cadettes. This occurred when I was in the sixth grade. We wore dark green skirts and white blouses, green hats, green badge sashes, pins, and other awards.

Cadette Level

Campcraft
Homemaker
Good Grooming

Extra Awards

Star of Bethlehem
Gold Three Leaf Clover
Brownie Girl Scout Wings
Patrol Leader Cord
Six Years of Stars
Sign of the Star
Sign of the Arrow
Circle T Council (from Ft. Worth. Texas in 1965)

During each meeting, we broke up into groups with the leaders and assistants to review our badge progress. With each step satisfactorily completed, they signed off in our handbooks. At the end of the year, a ceremonial award dinner was held at the church. We were presented with the badges in front of our parents and siblings.

At least once a year, the Girl Scouts held a Father Daughter Banquet. This was a highly anticipated time for all the girls. Menus were planned, and personal invitations were handwritten for the special man in each scout's life.

The girls provided the entertainment once the meal was complete. I particularly loved learning to sing, "Are You Sleeping, Are You Sleeping, Brother John?" We were divided into groups to memorize the song in several different languages. Terri's group learned the German words, and my group learned the French words. Terri and I were fascinated with the challenge. We giggled quite a lot making the activity a little verbal duel between us. The big evening arrived, and after the meal, the singers headed for the stage.

"Are You Sleeping, Brother John?"

(English)

Are you sleeping, are you sleeping?
Brother John, Brother John,
Morning bells are ringing, morning bells are ringing
Ding Ding Dong, Ding Ding Dong.

(French)

Frere Jacques, Frere Jacques
Dormez vous? Dormez vous?
Sonnes les matines, sonnez les matines,
Din, dan, don. Din, dan, don.

(German)

Bruder Jakob, Bruder Jakob,
Schläfst du noch? Schläfst du noch?
Horst du nicht die Glocken, hörst du nicht die Glocken?
Ding dang dong, ding dang dong.

(Spanish)

¿Estás dormido?,
¿estás dormido?
Hermano John,
¿hermano John?
Las campanas de la mañana están sonando,
las campanas de la mañana están sonando,
ding, dang, dong, ding, dang, dong.

The finale was an intricate joyful blending of all the different versions in rounds. The girls were ecstatic as the faces in the audience burst into big smiles. The dads were pretty proud of their daughters, making the evening a precious memory!

On a very sunny Saturday morning, Terri, as a Brownie, and I, as a Junior, participated in a very patriotic celebration! Both the Boy Scouts and the Girl Scouts who met at Grace Lutheran Church participated in a Scout Parade. Everyone was dressed in full uniform, the boys in their various shades of blue and khaki, and the girls in brown, green, and white. Leaders were dressed in their uniforms according to the levels and the groups to which they belonged. We met on the ball field between Concord Lutheran School and the Pagedale Police Department. Terri and I were both appointed flag bearers. All such enlisted carried large red, white and blue American flags or scout flags. Most of us had not experienced such an activity. The sheer beauty and pride of children in parade formation around the field was heartwarming nonetheless.

52 – Crafts and Needlework

Creativity was instilled in my heart at an early age. In many ways this was planted by my mother who was very detailed and saw value in taking the necessary amount of time to complete each task. She told me that anything worth doing, was worth doing right. That is one encouragement that continues to ring in my ears to this day and when I heed it, all is well.

Mom was very talented with needle and thread. She sewed, embroidered, and crocheted. One of my earliest recollections is her sitting at the kitchen table at night, working on her projects when Dad was traveling.

Embroidering became one of her favorite past-times, and she taught us how to cross-stitch and how to make French knots. She also crocheted edging on handkerchieves for ladies. Handkerchieves were used by men, women, and children. They were very popular before the wide use of tissues. Dad had a couple dozen that Mom washed and ironed for him continually. They were plain white. Mom's "hankies" were smaller and more delicate; just right for the fine trim she crocheted with variegated colored threads. She sold quite a few of them. I was especially fond of the ones with green and black trim.

Mom's enjoyment of needlecraft led me to appreciate fabric and yarns as a young child. Once on a visit to Grandma's house, we were given a dollar each and told we could go "uptown" by ourselves to spend it. I must have been about ten. Terri and I went to a dime store in the town square in Searcy. I bought some variegated green yarn. I really had no idea what to do with it, but I was very proud of it. Eventually, I used it to make an octopus doll with braided legs.

On one vacation, we took an interest in trinkets from the ocean. Mom bought collage kits for us. They had boards covered with burlap and a good variety and number of shells and some dried seaweed. It was interesting to see the many different beautiful colors and patterns God created.

We successfully explored paint by numbers, weaving potholders, and making pom-poms. Unsuccessfully, we tried knitting. Mom did not know how to do it, and none of us could understand the directions.

Mom kept all her sewing supplies on the bottom shelf of the built-in corner cabinet in the kitchen. Her big black Domestic Sewing Machine, with its many attachments, was her pride and joy. She had notions (thread, bobbins, buttons, pin cushion, tape measure, seam ripper, pattern tracing wheel, scissors, etc.), which she stored in a red cookie tin with a white lid. A repurposed Sucrets® tin held straight pins and needles. A boxed pair of pinking shears, the iron, patterns, fabric, and other creative delights armed Mom, a very talented seamstress, for the battle of making and maintaining a good majority of her daughters' wardrobes and costumes.

She made all kinds of play clothes and simple dresses for us. She pulled out her patterns and fabric, purchased at JCPenney®, and prepared several projects at a time. Once she had placed out the material and pinned and cut out the patterns for each outfit, she stacked them in a big pile. She could be more productive that way.

Seersucker fabric was trendy in the mid 1960s. It was a cotton fabric woven into striped or plaid designs consisting of puckered and flat sections. Mom chose several pastel colors with alternating white stripes. This meant that she could use white thread for all of the garments she was making. Shorts, tops, and summer dresses, called "shifts," flew off of the bed of her sewing machine, giving us several outfits to wear. She did a superb job and we enjoyed the clothes she made for us. I especially liked the fresh looking celery-green and white seersucker she used for my shift.

All this exposure to Mom's sewing and the knowledge that Grandma was a terrific seamstress, prompted me to pursue these skills. I asked Grandma if she could teach me to sew but she redirected me to ask Mom. I probably had not thought of asking for her before because she usually sewed when we girls were away from the house or asleep.

Upon Grandma's recommendation, and when I was in third grade, Mom let me buy a pattern for making Barbie® doll clothes. She wanted me to figure it all out by myself. I was so frustrated! She said, "Just follow the directions!" For a child unfamiliar with sewing terminology, they were not much more useful than guidelines written in Martian.

I did what I thought they were telling me to do, pinning the pattern to the fabric and cutting it out. It did not make much sense to me, as there were no instructions saying to remove pattern pieces before sewing, so I stitched the coordinating pieces together including the pattern!

Mom then realized that some one on one instruction was greatly needed. She taught me some of the basics without using patterns. That was so much more helpful. She was very particular, and I ripped out more than I sewed. Yet, in the end, I appreciated the lessons I used the rest of my life, as much as if not more than the projects completed.

I learned another lesson that significantly portrayed the importance to do things right. Mom decided to complete several summer outfits for herself and her daughters before an upcoming vacation. In her haste to conquer the task before the looming departure date, she took a short cut and not wash the fabric before cutting and sewing the garments. This one relaxation of her standards resulted in dense dust and fabric treatment accumulation in the sewing machine. This infected her eyelids and she developed carbuncles. Not being able to overcome the pain, she ended up in the doctor's office to have her eyelids lanced. After several weeks, her eyes healed and she was able to resume her sewing once more. It was a horrible thing for her to go through and a lesson none of us forgot. Thank you, Mom for your sacrifices for us! They were greatly appreciated.

Musical Interlude

53 - Opposing Dreams

In the spring of my fifth-grade year, the school began offering band lessons in the cafeteria. A gentleman involved in music at the Gas Light Square was hired to be the teacher, and my parents excitedly registered me into the class. When they queried me on my choice of the instruments, I quickly responded, "piano, drums or flute!" That got me excited!

The day arrived when they came back from the music store and proudly presented me with — none of my choices! I opened the caramel-colored hard case to find something I had never seen or heard of before. It was in four pieces and was black and silver. I was informed that it was a clarinet and I was going to love playing it! I did not buy that story for a minute and asked why they did not get one of the three instruments I was interested in. They said piano is not a band instrument, and drums were too noisy. The man at the store had convinced them that I probably did not have enough wind to play the flute! Really??? Then the real reason surfaced. Dad loved a clarinet player named Acker Bilk. The problem was that I had never heard of him, nor did I remember Dad ever mention Acker Bilk or clarinets before. So there it was!

Every week for the next year and a half, I dragged that clarinet to school and took the classes. I did not know how to read music to play an instrument, and evidently, neither did my parents. The teacher did not take much time to help me understand what I was supposed to do. I began to watch the boy sitting next to me and place my fingers where he did on his silver clarinet. That worked for a while. Then the lessons moved on to sharps and flats, and that did me in. I did not want to tell my parents about my confusion. I just could not break my dad's heart. Mom endured my horrible practicing but eventually told me I had practiced enough.

The clarinet was passed through all three girls in the family. Eventually, it was sold to a pawn shop by my mother about seven years later. By the way, we never had one recording by Acker Bilk for some reason. Funny, as I am writing this, 53 years later, my curiosity finally was stirred to check him out. Well, you know the old saying, "Better late than never!" Hmm, he was really pretty good!

54 - More About Music

$\mathcal{M}$r. Herbert Toensing had a three-fold influence on my life. He not only taught at the school but also was the organist, choir director, and orchestra director for Grace Lutheran Church and the director of the St. Louis Lutheran Children's Choir. I was blessed to sit under his instruction in three different choirs. I dearly loved his masterful ability to convey the love of God and His powerful nature through music. At church, he played the organ so well that your heart was moved, and the melodies echoed in the recesses of your mind for life. He was an excellent teacher and leader for the choirs and musicians. Requiring our intense concentration, he taught us to watch his lips to enunciate each word clearly as we sang. His eyes seemed to sparkle as he drew voluminous sounds of praises to God from the strings of our hearts and souls or the softest of whispers with a look, a facial expression, or a simple gesture of his hands or baton. He had an exceptional ability to convey the character qualities of discipline and appreciation.

The St. Louis Lutheran Children's Choir was made up of children from Lutheran churches and schools from all over the area. On a Saturday morning in the fall of 1963, my father took me to St. Stephen's Lutheran Church and School on Olive and Boyle in the old Gaslight Square area. Being in the fifth grade, I was old enough for the tryout. All of the potential choir members were taken to a brightly sunlit room with a grand piano. The pianist took each of us individually, played notes, and asked us to match them with our voices. He told me that I had a two-and-a-half-octave range and that I sang a little on the sharp side, but he passed me anyway and assigned me to the first soprano section.

Once the testing was completed and our voice assignments were made, we were sent to the large choir room upstairs. It was a much more somber looking room with its dark wooden floors and had less natural light than the tryout room. Eighty-some chairs were set in rows in a semi-circular arrangement. A grand piano anchored the room on one side, and a podium was placed in front of the chairs so that all eyes could easily follow the choir director. We met with the choir members, the accompanist, Mr. Victor Freudenburg, and the director, Mr. Toensing. I was very excited when I saw him in front of the room, as I highly respected him. From then on, every Saturday, we met from nine to noon to learn the songs that we were to present for Christmas and spring concerts.

Several weeks before each concert, we brought our lunches and stayed until three in the afternoon. We learned to sing in parts, and as we needed more practice, each section of the choir was given the specific time to master their parts. Mr. Toensing then wove all our voices into an audible tapestry perfectly blended for the final performances. Experiencing the effect of such hard work and discipline is a jewel in the setting of life.

Twelve of the students from Concord Lutheran School tried out and were accepted. They represented the Lutheran Churches, St. Andrews, Grace (Pagedale), St. James, and Unity (Belnor). The Thirteenth Annual Spring Concert given April 12th, 1964, included seventy-one choir members from twenty Lutheran churches in the St. Louis area. My two favorite songs from that concert were:

"Ride the Chariot,"
and
"Give Me Your Tired, Your Poor."

In the Fourteenth Annual Spring Concert given on May 9th, 1965, twenty-two Lutheran churches and three Lutheran schools were represented by seventy choir members. My favorite songs from this concert were:

"O Word of God Incarnate,"
"Climbing Jacob's Ladder,"
"Tum Balalay Ka,"
"Skip to My Lou,"
and
"You're a Grand Old Flag."

Spring concerts were held at Salem-Afton School Auditorium, 8343 Gravois at 4 p.m. and Lutheran High School Auditorium, Lake and Waterman at 7 p.m. That made for long days, but we loved it!

I was in the Christmas Candlelight Concerts in the years 1963 and 1964. Unfortunately, my copy of 1963 concert program was lost years ago, and I can no longer remember what we sang. In both years, two performances were given in a beautiful old church, also named Grace Lutheran Church. It was located at St. Louis and Garrison. The interior of the church was furnished with darker colored pews. It had an enormous pipe organ mounted in the balcony over the pulpit and altar area.

We wore long black choir robes with a contrasting white shorter overgarment. Both the Lutheran Hour Choir and the St. Louis Lutheran Children's Choir sang in these programs. Some of the songs were sung with the combined choirs, but we also sang separately. The choirs could not see each other during the program as we were in different locations in the sanctuary.

In 1964, the prelude of Handel's Adagio and Andante (G-minor Organ Concerto) was played. Reverend G. E. Nitz gave the opening prayer and remarks. The dimly lit church increased the anticipation of both choirs entering through the narthex doors of the church. They made their way down the side and middle aisles, walking in pace with the music and carrying battery-operated candles. In the processional, we sang:

"Let Us All with Gladsome Voice,"
"O Come All Ye Faithful,"
and
"Good Christian Men Rejoice."

As the older choir filled their places, the children's choir approached the two stairways on either side of the altar area that led to the choir loft. By the end of the processional, the front of the church was filled with beautiful voices and candlelight. The sanctuary lights were brightened, and both choirs and congregation joined in singing the Christmas hymns:
"It Came Upon a Midnight Clear,"
"O Little Town of Bethlehem,"
and
"Silent Night".

Next, the Lutheran Hour Choir sang:
"When Morning Gilds the Skies
and
a medley of carols which included
"Joy to the World,"
"The First Noel,"
"Lo, How a Rose E'er Blooming,"
"O Come, All Ye Faithful"
and
"O Thou Joyous Day."

The musical tapestry continued with the combined choirs singing

"Christmas Roundelay"

followed by the children singing:

"O Little Town of Bethlehem,"
"O Nightingale Awake,"
and
"Come all Ye Shepherds."

The older choir continued with:

"Babe of Beauty"
"All My Heart This Night Rejoices,"
and
"Before the Paling of the Stars."

The children responded with:

"Rejoice and Be Glad,"
"God Rest You Merry Gentlemen,"
and
"As It Fell Upon a Night."

Dr. E. R. Bertermann gave the sermon. Afterward, "In Dulci Jubilo" by Buxtehude was played as the voluntary. The combined choirs then sang:

"From Heights of Heaven to Earth I Fare,"
and
"The Noel Carol."

The recessional hymns followed:

"Let Us All with Gladsome Voice,"
"O Come All Ye Faithful,"
and
"Good Christian Men Rejoice!"

The prayer and benediction followed with the postlude of Bach's

"In Thee is Gladness."

Then all were released to go back out into the world filled with the message of our Savior on our hearts and our minds. How wonderful, how marvelous to spend a few hours consumed and wrapped in that message. Nothing mattered more. Much joy filled those candlelit walls. Being able to lift our voices as a gift of praise to God, and His wonderful gift of His Son, the Messiah Jesus Christ, shared with those who attended that evening, was precious for all concerned. The memories of those concerts continue to wrap my heart with God's love and bring gentle tears of gratefulness to my eyes.

Summer Vacation 1964

55 – The Way of the Winds

*O*ur vacation in August of 1964 was bursting at the seams with not only the familiarity of past semi-annual excursions to the northeast but also embellished with special surprises woven into the fabric. However, the first memory was basked in the fever of frustration.

We loaded into that beautiful but non-air-conditioned Palomar Red 1964 Chevrolet Impala with its black interior, huge trunk, and ample seating early in the morning after Mom made sure everything in the house was in good order. Patience was never a strong suit in our family, so the delay began our start with an essence of irritation. Hastily, our journey started by passing the Gateway Arch, still under construction, and crossing the Mississippi River into Illinois.

By the time we were almost out of Indiana, we were all a bit cranky since we skipped breakfast to get on the road six hours earlier. Dad's lunch destination was somewhere in the vicinity of Ohio. Apparently, he wanted to take us to a unique local restaurant. When we arrived, it was packed to the gills, and a long line of people were waiting for tables. Dad added our names to the list, and after a lengthy interval, we were finally seated at a table far in the back near the kitchen. The seating hostess must have had a communication breakdown with the waitresses because no one came to take our orders nor give us water. We obviously had been overlooked in the chaos. After we waited for what Dad calculated to be an hour, which was far longer than his patience and hunger could endure, he stood up. With his booming voice, he requested how long we would have to wait to get service. The rest of us were not only tired and hungry but now mortified by the experience. With that, all the activity in the restaurant came to a screeching halt. Dad told us to gather our belongings and marched us through the stunned and whispering employees and patrons and out the front door. The distance seemed to increase exponentially to a minimum of what seemed like a mile. We returned to the car, and not a word was spoken for quite a while.

Eventually, we made it to the usual stop at Aunt Kay's and family in Trumansburg, New York. Patti was now engaged, so we met her fiancé. Terri and I were old enough to ride bikes into the town and visit a little store for postcards and treats. She remembers going to a field to see horses. On our return, we took a sharp corner. Terri lost control and slid across the finely crushed gravel, embedding some into her bare leg. I felt so bad, and she did not think that she could make it back without help. I hated leaving her but raced back to the house. Someone in the family quickly responded. They brought her home, tended to her wounds, and she was soon hard at play. On the weekend, we picnicked at the Finger Lakes once more. The visit was short and ended with watching Jimmy's football team hold a skirmish on the field behind the house. That was the first time I had ever seen football. It was something never watched or mentioned at home. I could not then, nor even now, understand the need for opponents smashing into each other and considering it fun. Of course, not being exposed to brothers would limit that experience. All the boys seemed to be having a terrific time, though. After lunch, we were on our way to Hazleton, Pennsylvania.

Aunt Anna and Uncle John had a new baby girl. Her name was Cheryl, and she was another cutie pie. We were only there for a few hours and headed for Reading, Pennsylvania. At the time, we girls did not understand that Dad was being considered for a position in the area. We did not go by the office but saw some of the sights, including a seven-story red pagoda at the top of Mount Penn, built in 1907. It stood high above the city, offering a magnificent panoramic view.

Our next stop was Philadelphia, where our visits were strategically organized to fit in as much as possible. Interlaced with visits with Mom's relatives and friends were tours to see our national treasures.

Mom's stepsister and best friend and her husband were the first on the list. While we were there, some street vendors were pushing carts on the sidewalks, offering fresh hot pretzels, and mustard and others offered Italian Water Ice. I loved the hot soft pretzels, an unexpected surprise, and very delicious. Next, we visited with Grandad and Uncle Pork for a few hours and then Uncle Deitz in the early evening. These were all short but sweet visits.

We visited Liberty Square, where we saw the Liberty Bell and toured Independence Hall. The tour included a view of the room where the Continental Congress met before and during the Revolutionary War. There they drafted, debated, and signed The Declaration of Independence in 1776. In 1787, The Constitution of the United States was established in the same room. It was quite an experience to realize that the history of the beginning of our country was put into effect in that very building. I remember trying to imagine what it must have been like during those days. On the second floor, a large harpsichord lay open at the end of the long hall. What a treat to see such a beautiful instrument. It had a double row of keys. We were told its unusual sound came from plucking the strings rather than striking them. Amazing.

Afterwards, we walked to Betsy Ross's tiny two-story home and learned more about the history of the American Flag. We climbed the narrow staircase whose steps were not very deep. They had a bed warmer displayed on Betsy's bed. A bed warmer was a metal pan on a long handle with a lid where hot coals were placed. It was stuck under the mattress for heat during cold nights.

A trip to a pier followed, as Dad had been in the Navy and his ship docked in Philadelphia during World War II. While he was on shore leave, he met Mom. They had corresponded for a few years, and when the war was over, Dad married her in February of 1946 while on furlough.

Two destinations filled the next day's calendar. Now to this point, I have refrained from sharing the full names of family members. This name was too much fun to ignore. Mom repeated it over and over again until it rang in our minds like a song. Here it is, "Minnie Syvilla Mae Hoffsommer Munroe." She was Great Grandma's baby sister and a very tiny lady! Aunt Minnie's stature was in complete contrast with her larger-than-life cheerfulness. Meeting her was just as delightful as learning her name, and she gave the biggest hugs! Dad wanted to take Terri and me to see the Philadelphia Mint, so Mom and Kim stayed with Aunt Minnie for the duration. It was a toss-up in my emotions to miss the afternoon visit with our Great Aunt Minnie, but Dad insisted, and off we went.

The tour of the mint was very educational. A large hall above the floor where the coins were struck was lined with large thick windows. That day they were allowing us to see pennies being made. I could not even imagine how many pennies I was seeing at one time. The copper coins were very bright and highly polished, not like those I was accustomed to seeing. The guide shared a great deal of technical information on the tour. More than seeing the actual mint, I enjoyed the excitement in Dad's eyes as he explained all that was taking place. After the tour ended, we stopped at a window where he purchased several newly minted coins, proof sets and uncirculated sets. Then we returned to Aunt Minnie's house for a short visit and to pick up Mom and Kim and head for the motel by the airport.

Before sunrise, we were on our way to the New York World's Fair! One hundred twenty-five miles later, New York City's impressive skyline was in our view. It was sad that we had no time to take in the sights because our schedule only allowed one day. Once inside the fair, the first thing to grab our attention was a walkway lined with the flags of countries from all over the world. It led to a twelve-story-high model of the earth called the Unisphere surrounded by beautiful water fountains. It was the symbol of the fair.

The Space Park exhibited a full-scale Saturn V Boattail and many other replicas. Sinclair Oil had a dinosaur display with life-size models. Disney had two attractions we visited. It's a Small World was an indoor boat ride through displays of mechanically moving doll-like figures representing nations far and wide. It was a beautifully friendly appearing exhibit. The tune was a little too catchy, and once heard, rang in your memory forever. Progressland was a circular display around which the audience was seated in sections of a revolving floor. Each set of the center stage chronologically displayed an audio-animatronic family throughout different periods during the twentieth century. The father acted as host and carried on conversations with his family and explained the details of the technology they experienced to make their lives better. The theme song was repeated at each point of time, convincing the audience that each advancement in technology and customs was indeed progress.

Several automobile companies, including Chrysler Corporation and General Motors, displayed their latest models in very futuristic pavilions. Ford introduced the Mustang. Beautiful water fountains, flags, and flowers were set all over the grounds. RCA debuted color television, and Bell brought us into the technology of the picture-phone. The scent of food from all around the world wafted through the air. Rides included people-movers, passenger-pods, monorails, and even an eighty-feet-high Ferris wheel appearing as a humongous tire by U.S. Royal. We saw many people who appeared to be famous or delegates from all over the world. Many wore official sashes and were accompanied by guides and guards. It was so exciting! One of the side vendors was an artist who lightly carved silhouettes on copper foil. Mom had the artist make impressions of each of us, and they decorated the walls of our homes for years.

Late in the afternoon, Dad took us to a souvenir shop and told us to pick out something to help us remember the fair. I looked and looked and looked but had a decidedly trying time choosing a memento. Dad, anxious to see as much as possible, tried to hurry me to make my decision so that we could go on. I just could not do it. Finally, he understood there was something to my struggle and asked, "What is the matter?"

I looked up into his eyes and started to cry. I said, "Daddy, I am afraid that we will not have enough money to get back home!" He gently escorted me out the door and around to the back of the shop. He pulled out his wallet and opened it and said, "Do you think this will get us home?" There was more money in that wallet than I could imagine!

I looked up at him with my tear-stained face and said, "Yes, Daddy!" He told me with a great deal of compassion, "Now I want you to go back in and pick out two souvenirs to take home!" I chose a beautiful white headscarf with an inch-and-a-half-wide red stripe around the edges. It depicted several of the different exhibits and had "New York World's Fair" written across its center. Secondly, I picked out a silver-toned metal bank with important sights from New York City embossed on the sides. About thirty years ago, I made a memory book for Dad for his birthday. When I handed him my bank, he looked at me and said that he could not take it. I said, "Then just hold it for me, and I'll get it back from you someday!" He did, and it stayed on his bookshelf until he went home to be with Jesus in 1993. Tonight, as I write, that bank is displayed on top of my bookshelf across the room.

Another father daughter bonding moment occurred in the morning when we got back to our motel. We arrived at about four o'clock in the morning. Kim and Terri had fallen asleep in the car, so they were carried in, and Mom got them ready for bed. We were getting settled, and Dad said, "Jilene, come with me!"

Out the door and into the car we went, and before I knew it, we were cruising the downtown streets looking for an all-night diner! Mom loved hoagie sandwiches, and Philadelphia had the best in the world! In fact, when she returned from her step-mother Mary's funeral back in 1961, she took an empty suitcase with her and had it filled with hoagies for her return flight. Therefore, Dad determined the culinary delights worth the pursuit in the wee morning hours. We found a very lively diner and perched on a couple of stools at the counter. The place was bursting with light and activity. The noise of laughter and chatter filled the air along with banging restaurant equipment and waitresses taking orders from patrons.

There was a mixture of the hurriedness of people leaving for work after a quick breakfast, and in stark contrast, there was the weariness of others coming off the night shifts to relax with a cup of coffee and donuts before heading home. The aroma of short-order eggs, toast, and bacon, pots of coffee, and Italian spices for sandwiches, roast beef dinners, and so forth encroached deliciously on our salivary senses. The waitress took our order for Italian hoagies complete with large Italian rolls, olive oil, red wine vinegar, ham, salami, capocolla, provolone cheese, shredded lettuce, sliced onion, tomatoes, pepperoncini, salt, pepper, and oregano. From the counter, we watched the cook assemble our food. Curled up on the stool next to my dad's side, I could see the pure delight in his smiling eyes as we awaited our order. The experience of being at the diner at five o'clock in the morning gave me a taste of a significant part of the lives of the citizens of "Philly." We returned to the motel, hoagies in hand, and I was so tired I do not remember eating them, but I went to sleep cradled in the love I had received that day!

56 - Southward
and
Westward Home

Our whirlwind vacation led us south, crossing the northern tip of Delaware on our way into Maryland. Two hours later, our first underwater experience was the Baltimore Harbor Tunnel. Dad made such a big to-do about us being under the water that we were quite nervous over the mile-and-a-half ordeal. The light at the end was quite welcomed. Within the next hour, we caught our first glimpse of Washington, D.C. Dad was certainly full of surprises!

We drove on west through the city and crossed the Potomac River. The Iwo Jima Memorial was a sobering sight. Its portrayal of the Marines in battle trying to raise the flag on Japanese soil made me cry as we were told the story of what took place near the end of World War II. Arlington Cemetery was next. My heart ached as we saw thousands of white headstones set at the final resting places across the rolling hills of beautiful green lawns. The sacrifice of so many men and women who had given their lives serving our country was overwhelming. We learned that the first military burial occurred after the Civil War. (May 13, 1864). We stood silently and watched the guards of the Tomb of the Unknown Soldier. Our parents explained that it held the remains of unidentified military men who had lost their lives during World War I, World War II, and the Korean Conflict. Dad's father had served in WWI, and Dad had served in both WWII and the Korean Conflict. Both were in the United States Navy. Painful memories haunted him as they do all persons who have faced war. This, too, was a profoundly somber honor to watch.

Because we had just lost President Kennedy to the assassination on the prior November 22nd, we came to his grave to pay our respects. An eternal flame was set there, and a white picket fence surrounded the site. That also was all too freshly painful a sight to see.

With heavy hearts, we left Arlington and continued toward the Lincoln Memorial. We climbed the stairs of the marble structure. Standing before the statue of a man who had weathered so much while leading our country through the civil war, we could not imagine what weight he carried in his heart. We pondered again at what price freedom comes. Reading Lincoln's Second Inaugural Address on the northern wall and the Gettysburg Address on the southern wall gave us a glimpse into the great pain, loss, and grief of those times. The weight of the entire memorial itself could not compare with the anguish he and our entire country faced.

The Washington Memorial honoring our first president was only seen from a distance. Climbing its inner staircase was not to be experienced. It was far too much for our family to take on that day.

The Jefferson Memorial was our next destination. Thomas Jefferson was one of the United States' founding fathers and the primary author of the Declaration of Independence. As it was late and already overwhelmed by the emotions experienced earlier that day, our visit within its walls only briefly touched on the president's work.

The next morning, putting on our "wings," we flew headlong into the day's activities. The sighting of the White House behind the tall black wrought-iron fence as we drove by teased our curiosity as to what was inside and the thoughts of missing a sighting of President Johnson.

We drove past the U.S. Capitol and many other impressive buildings as Dad honed in on his target, the Smithsonian Institute. Our visit to three of the nine museums was akin to glimpsing hors d'oeuvres from the halls of a massive banquet being held in a series of over-abundantly stocked storehouses. In the National Air and Space Museum, we sighted many airplanes, including the "Wright Flyer", which was the first plane to be flown by Wilbur and Orville Wright dating back to December 1903. "The Spirit of St. Louis" was the first airplane to cross the Atlantic Ocean. It was flown by Charles A. Lindbergh on May 20th-21st, 1927, from New York to Paris, France. (My Dad was two and a half years old, and Mom was two months old at that time.) As someone born in St. Louis, I could not help but sense a little bit of pride. Outside were several exhibits from the space program.

We raced to the National Museum of Natural History, passing animal exhibits, including dinosaurs. Our destination was the Hall of Geology, Gems, and Minerals to view the 45-carat-plus Hope Diamond at Mom's insistence. As impressive as this precious blue gemstone was, it was not as beautiful and sparkly as I had supposed it would be. However, in the new Museum of History and Technology, the display of the gowns of first ladies set in rooms corresponding with the president's time in office was quite a feast for the eyes of any girl, young or old. Even so, the details remained a blur. The year 1964 was also the first year the massive 30-feet by 42-feet Star-Spangled Banner was on display. It was the inspiration for Francis Scott Key's writing the words that became our national anthem as a result of the American victory over the British in the

Battle of Baltimore at Ft. McHenry on September 14th, 1814. Washington, D.C.; what an amazing two days!

Dad was on a roll, and early the next morning, we took to the highway west into Virginia. The jewels of this day's excursion were seen in little more than an hour. We entered the Blue Ridge Mountains and took the Skyline Drive. Stopping on several occasions, we were fascinated by the vastly beautiful views both above and below us. The crisp, clean air added to the moment, and I was surprised to be slipping into my car coat to warm up on an August morning.

The vast beauty of the blue drenched sky, the deep summer green of the trees, and the grass-covered mountains took the appearance of heaps of emeralds and peridots woven into a breathtaking tapestry.

We stopped at a restaurant and gift shop in Skyland in Luray. Given a chance to pick up a souvenir, I was ready and eagerly picked out the one and only pocket knife I ever had. It was about two inches long with two blades and a mother of pearl handle. "Blue Ridge Parkway" was engraved on its side. How often that little knife brought back memories and issued new ones.

Laden with our purchases, we returned to the Impala to enjoy the many winding roads and views along the way. The good feeling of the cool breezes crossing the interior of the car was very welcomed. In light of the fact we had spent so much time receiving the hair-tangling high winds on the highway, they were quite a blessing. The trip through the high mountains and the low valleys remained as engraved on my mind as much as the road was carved through the landscape we visited.

Early evening brought us to the house of the friends from school and church who had moved to Virginia at the beginning of summer. Their son was in my class at school for a few years. Before they left St. Louis, his mother had given my mom a charming cream-colored ceramic coffee pot decorated with brown designs. A music box that played the song, "Let's Have Another Cup of Coffee," was built into its base. Mom often turned the key and reminisced about their friendship, so it was a highly anticipated treat to visit them. They were the family who hosted the New Year's Eve party, where the intoxicated man had destroyed the three parked cars, including Dad's brand new 1962 Ford Fairlane 500. In all, many memories were shared between the adults, and we certainly enjoyed seeing them again that evening.

The morning light faced us with the waning hours of our massively filled vacation. The plan was to leave Virginia, crossing through West Virginia, Kentucky, Indiana, Illinois crossing the Mississippi River at St. Louis and home to Wellston. Little did we know that along our path would come a severe storm that led to a fatal accident on a bridge we were to cross. The traffic was gridlocked for hours at the impassible two-lane highway. God's timing is perfect, and more often than not, we are little aware of all that is happening around us. Delays such as these can bring our hearts to pray for all involved and praise Him for the protection of those spared. That is a concept that I had yet to learn.

Finally, our eyes were fixed on the two stainless steel legs of the unfinished Gateway Arch. Crossing the Mississippi River, we were within half an hour's reach of our home. Uninterrupted time spent together as a family experiencing things that none of us had seen before was such a blessing. Even if I never spoke of it then, it was one of the most moving and happy times of my life.

Our parents' perspective was a stark realization of opposite ends of a pole. Mom loved going through the different sites that we visited on these vacations, and we girls would have loved to linger at them a little longer. On the other hand, Dad had more of an attitude of conquering the list of destinations rather than enjoying them. So vacations became more a matter of flipping through the pages of life than reading between the lines. By the time I was twelve, I could say that I had been to twenty of the fifty states.

We pulled up alongside the house, grabbed what was necessary, and climbed the steps of our home sweet home. The rest of the unpacking could wait for the morrow. Soon, we plunged into our own beds, curling into the blankets and pillows. Moments later, I was reliving highlights of our incredible adventures in my mind until my eyelids slowly closed like curtains at the end of a delightfully moving play. Contentment wrapped its loving arms around me, and I comfortably drifted into the dreams of the past few weeks.

Transitions

57 – Unrest Permeates Our Lives

The fall of 1964 began, and with it, a little unrest had subtly woven itself into the fabric of our family life. Mom and Dad pretty much kept the details to themselves. Still, we could not get away from the underlying feelings of apprehension.

Dad had been working with American Casualty Company since about 1955. A fire damaged the St. Louis office sometime in the early 1960s. After it was deemed safe to enter, he had us accompany him to show the damage done to the building. We entered the main floor, which days before bustled with employees and clients busily conducting their business, the sounds of typewriters, telephones, and other business machines. Now it was eerily quiet, damp and dark, and the smell of smoke still lingered in the air. Dad led us up the stately designed wooden staircase to the second floor. He pointed out the fire damage and the water damage from the sprinklers and fire hoses, carefully steering us away from dangerous areas. At the end of the long hallway was the casualty and underwriting department, where Dad had his office. He continued to expound on fire safety and soon gathered surviving files he needed for his next business trip. As he escorted us back to the car, I thought about the people that worked in the building and how hard it must have been for them. It was an unforgettable experience to see the aftermath of the fire. Still, I appreciated Dad's safety consciousness and desire to point out so many dangers surrounding us.

American Casualty Company, whose headquarters were in Reading, Pennsylvania, was sold in 1963. It was merged with Continental Casualty Company, based in Chicago, and National Fire Insurance Company of Hartford. Eventually, the newly formed company was named Continental National American Group, simply known as CNA. Dad's position was swallowed up in the merger, and he was transferred to Reading.

We were used to him being gone four or five days at a time, but he was always home on the weekends. Now he was gone a month or more at a time. Phone calls, being very expensive, were few and short in length. Letters became our form of communication. Mom was excited about the possibility of moving near Philadelphia, where she grew up, but the thought of leaving the only home we girls remembered caused some anxiousness.

In anticipation of a move to Pennsylvania, our parents listed the house with a real estate agent. It was a difficult time to sell a home. This, of course, brought more stress to Dad and Mom.

In the meantime, we girls, being eleven, nine, and five years old, continued our activities with school, Girl Scouts, church, choir, and band. Up until then, Mom had never felt the need to learn to drive as public transportation stopped right in front of our house. If we could not go by bus, we relied on our friends. One of those friends was Mrs. Downes, who had a daughter about our age. She drove a white-and-light-blue car, which she called the "blue goose." Mom was on her bowling team. Once a week, the moms and children piled into her car and headed for the bowling alley on Ferguson Avenue south of Page Boulevard. The bowlers were dressed in their white blouses with forest-green embroidered advertising of the team sponsor and matching forest-green skirts. As they met their team at the lanes, the children stole away to the attached restaurant. If we could get Mom to agree, we passed the time eating hamburgers and fries and drinking sodas. It seemed that we spent many hours there each week, and it helped to have the company of other children.

Another thing that filled our time while Dad was away was shopping trips. We rode as many as three city buses to our destinations. Before we left the house, Mom slipped a little handgun into her jacket pocket, grabbed Kim's hand, and the four of us marched to the bus stop. That scared the daylights out of me, but Mom was brave. (In 2014, we found that gun sitting on a window sill in her bedroom. We had it checked out only to discover that it was not a real weapon after all, but only a gun to start races. No bullets were required, but it could be used to scare an intruder.

58 - Sixth Grade

Sixth grade seemed in many ways a continuation of the previous year. The idea of having all the same teachers turned out to be a very stabilizing element for me. Everything seemed more exciting and happier. We took up where we left off before summer, but some new experiences were added.

Concord Lutheran School was made up of members from four different Lutheran churches in the area. One of the requirements for attending the school was maintaining regular church attendance. Therefore, the method of calling the roll in the school on Mondays was different than on the other days. Instead of saying, "Here," we were to answer "Yes" or "No" in response to the question of whether or not we attended church the day before.

On one Monday morning, there was a big difference in the atmosphere. The students were in the classroom in their seats awaiting roll call when Mr. McWhirter entered the room. He was very determined as he abruptly landed his books on his desk and turned his eyes on us in a manner that demanded our attention. He was adamant! He was courageous! What he said next would change my life forever! He told us that it did not matter who was preaching! What mattered was that we check what was being said with God's Word to make sure what was being said was right! I was eleven when he told us that. I had little idea at that point how to do what he said, but I never forgot what he said! The seed was planted deep enough in my spirit that it sprouted eighteen years later, when I learned how to study the Bible. Then I began to grow in ways I had never dreamed possible. This reminds me of the verse which says of the Bereans, "These were more noble than those in Thessalonica, in that they received the word with all readiness of mind, and searched the scriptures daily, whether those things were so." Acts 17:11, KJV[F].

One of the activities I enjoyed most often occurred at the end of the day. Mr. McWhirter had us pull out our hymnals and ask the students to give suggestions for which hymns to sing. I loved this time so much and was thrilled every time I was allowed to request my choice. We would leave after prayer with those hymns placed lovingly into our hearts and minds.

On January 6th, 1965, Concord Lutheran School held an Epiphany Concert at Grace Lutheran Church across the street. What a wonderful time it was! Of course, Mr. Toensing directed, and Pastor Biel officiated. Mrs. Joan Beit was the pianist and organist. Epiphany is the celebration of the wise men's visit to Jesus, Mary, and Joseph, when Jesus was about three years old. It signifies that Jesus had come for not only the Jewish people but also the non-Jewish people who are called Gentiles. There was an abundance of great music with this celebration. My two favorite pieces that we sang were "The Three Kings - Christmas Cantata for Epiphany" by Fritz Dietrich, and "Ho, Jeanette, Make Haste Isabella" (A French Carol).

After this service, most of the congregation crossed the street and headed for the field behind the school. People brought their undecorated Christmas trees with them for a celebratory bonfire. There was more singing, laughter, and joy. That year we had just studied the stars and the constellations in school. The stars shone so brightly that night. We could identify the constellation, Orion, which is mentioned in the book of Job in the Holy Bible! I was pretty excited about that also!

When all the trees were burned, some of the crowd stayed to make sure the fire was completely out, and everything was cleaned up. Families gathered their youngest children, deeply asleep from exhaustion. The rest were saying they did not want to go as they continued chasing each other some more. Everyone else chatted on, trying to finish the last bits of conversation before their departure. All those memories still burn in the hearts of many from the school and the church and are even talked about to this day. I recently was told by Mr. Meyermann's oldest daughter, Natalie, that he was the one who started the Epiphany bonfire custom. The entire evening was such a blessing!

At the end of the school year, a celebratory camping trip was given for the sixth-, seventh- and eighth-grade students. My parents let me attend, which was a milestone for me. I remember doing a little hiking, but my favorite thing, as usual, was the crafts. We were given small wooden trinket boxes to which we added bits of tile and grout to the lid. Of course, I inset a "J" in black bits in the center and was quite pleased with the results. I have hidden many a sweet treasure in that box over the years. Yes, I still have mine even though part of the lid was broken off and lost.

59 – The Last Summer in St. Louis

By April 1965, Mom's dreams of moving to Pennsylvania were shattered when Dad deemed himself incompatible with CNA's merger. Another insurance company offered to interview him, so he flew from Reading to Tulsa, Oklahoma. He then came home to regroup and work out the new plans. What an emotional turn of events for our parents!

On the night of his return, we were filled with joy to see him! It was already past bedtime when he arrived, and we were in our pajamas. That did not matter, and the hi-fi was cranked up, the movie camera loaded, and suddenly we were showing off the latest dance moves we had learned from watching tv.

That weekend he took us to downtown St. Louis to the Mississippi riverfront to catch a close-up view of the Jefferson National Expansion Memorial's progress. It is more often called the Gateway Arch and the Gateway Arch to the West. Construction began on February 12th, 1963. By early summer 1964, it had climbed high enough on the horizon that we could actually see it from our front yard on a clear day. It was quite interesting to note the progress from that vantage point. It had probably reached more than 450 feet of its 630 feet completed height by the time we got our first close-up view. It was a beautiful crisp windy spring day. We were bundled up in our fuzzy blue and red spring jackets. Dad posed us with our arms up in the air, making us appear as if we could reach as high as the incomplete legs of the monument. What fun to pretend such a thing. We all giggled at the thought. We viewed the signs of the proposed plans for the area and dreamed of one day visiting and going up to the top of the arch and shopping in its base in the gift stores.

Another noted site was the beginning of the construction of Busch Memorial Stadium or Busch Stadium II. The city broke ground on May 24th, 1964. It had already taken the appearance of the beginning shape of a Roman coliseum and promised to be quite a beautiful stadium. It was to replace the fifty-one-year-old Sportsman's Park, which was renamed Busch Stadium in 1953. We had tried to see the Cardinals play two different games over the years but both games were rained out.

The next week, Dad landed the job in Tulsa and returned to take us for a visit. Our Girl Scout Troops were having their year-end awards ceremony at the same time. I had become a patrol leader that year and felt the responsibility of being there with my group. I appealed to my parents to stay in St. Louis. Permission was granted, and the Stewart family was kind enough to let me stay with them for the duration. It was sad for me to go through the awards without the family there.

Come May, Dad returned home to take us all on a quick trip to Tulsa. We crossed the Missouri line into Oklahoma by way of the Will Rogers Turnpike. Halfway to Tulsa, we visited the famous Glass House Restaurant[9]. It was a unique experience as the structure was shaped like a steel arch, spanning the four lanes and wide median of the highway! Matching service stations anchored the parking lots for the fine dining restaurant. Patrons had a view of the passing traffic from seating beside the large arched windows. We did not eat there but enjoyed the visit, none-the-less.

Tulsa was a remarkably clean, beautiful, and windy city. The downtown area was well maintained and landscaped, and waste bins were on nearly every corner. We looked at houses and daydreamed about what it would be like to live there. We came across our first horned toad while we were house hunting. We had no problem heeding Dad's warning to steer clear of it.

One morning, we went to a local restaurant and had the best French toast ever made. The slices were at least an inch thick, battered in an egg mixture and lightly deep-fried. Butter, hot maple syrup, and powdered sugar enhanced the slices of melt in your mouth goodness.

Afterwards, we went shopping, and Mom bought new dresses for each of us. Mine was a beautiful dark pink coral color, double-breasted, reversible jumper with large matching buttons in two rows. A white long-sleeved blouse with a small flowery print completed the ensemble. I loved wearing it as it made me feel so cheerful.

Dad picked us up late in the afternoon. He took us out for dinner and to the slot car races. It was so much fun to be together again for a short few days. Once back home, Mom tried to keep things as normal as possible for us and began making her plans for the move.

Within the first few weeks of summer, Vacation Bible School was in session. It was particularly heart-moving to me that year as we studied the love of our suffering Savior. The craft we did amplified what I was feeling. We were given a piece of heavy green foil and a picture of Jesus praying leaning on a rock in Gethsemane. His face was looking up, crying out to His Father to remove the cup of suffering He was about to partake of. In the agony of sweating drops of blood, he added, "Not My will, but Thine be done!" That crudely crafted picture has had an ever-present effect on me all of my life, pointing out to me what is most important! God loved us so much that He was willing to send His Son to take the punishment for the sins of all who wanted to have a relationship with Him here and in eternity. I was just beginning to realize that faith was personal, not just a matter of attending church. I had so much more to learn. I did not know this was going to be my last Vacation Bible School.

Early evenings were filled with the softball schedule, practices, and games. Dad came home every weekend in time to coach. Of course, we relished that time. One evening, the team and their families gathered at ball diamonds across from Baerveldt Park on Ferguson Avenue between the Pagedale City Hall and Concord Lutheran School. A game was played between the moms and team members. Dads and siblings watched and cheered from the side. Many of us had never seen our moms swing a bat or catch a ball, let alone play a game. For the most part, the training of ballplayers seemed to be the unspoken job of the dads. Moms mostly made sure their daughters had everything they needed for each practice and game. They kept our uniforms clean and in order, cheered the players, made the refreshments, corralled the siblings, and bandaged the boo-boos. Some moms kept score, like our mom, and made calls when necessary. To see the moms in a totally different activity, actually being our adversaries, was astounding, to say the least. Dads were torn over what side they should cheer. The guarded quietness among them was a little comical. Most everyone knows that cheering your favorite team is serious business, but when you have to live in the same house with the opponents in a game, you must tread lightly. Good-natured teasing and abundant laughter filled the air despite the desperate seriousness of the actual game and the opponents. The memory of the victor and the score has entirely left me and really does not matter. It was a beautiful and heartwarming event enjoyed by all. I will say this, the moms gave it their best!

60 - Changing Winds

By the end of summer, the company Dad worked for also went through a merger. Thus, moving to Tulsa became a faded dream. He did not want to go through the uncertainty of the process since he was one of the youngest in seniority with the company. He sought out other companies seeking to hire underwriters. A position became available with Commercial Standard Insurance Company in Ft. Worth, Texas. Dad was warmly brought into their corral and expected to start in September 1965.

The winds of change were indeed blowing hard, directing us much further southwest to a wild land we had only "heard tell of" on television and in the westerns full of cattle and cowboys. Such were the pre-impressions in the mind of this then twelve-year-old girl.

Our parents had to make some hard and fast decisions as the house had not been sold, and we did not want to be apart when the new school year started. They hired a couple to come in and act as live-in managers of the property. Their responsibilities were keeping up with all the renters and the needs of the house. That was very hard for our parents as that type of arrangement does not often work for the good of the owners. Commercial Standard arranged for a moving company to ship our belongings to Ft. Worth. Because things happened so quickly, the family did not even have time to visit the new location before the move.

The softball teams got together and threw the most heart-warming party for us. The Metzners, Kochs, and Martins planned the joyful event, and there was an abundance of traditional potluck foods and beverages. The gathering was set as a season end party with awards for all of the girls. Someone operated the movie camera, and joy abounded as Dad gave each girl a certificate. Many of us had played softball together for four years, so some of the girls snuck in a quick hug when they received their rewards.

Finally, some parting speeches were made by a few of the parents and friends, and a beautiful white sheet cake was brought out. On the northeast edge, a sign of St. Louis was painted in the icing. A narrow road widened as it approached a sign labeled Ft. Worth in the southwest corner. A plastic car was set on the road heading that way with best wishes following close behind. What a precious gesture! What love we felt that evening as the final pages of our lives in St. Louis were drawing to an end.

Conclusion

*W*ithin days of the going-away party and the last time at church service, our belongings were packed and loaded onto the moving van. With each item leaving the house, the vacancy left behind shouted a silent cry of inevitable change and loneliness, stealing away my childhood memories.

The last item was loaded. The doors of the moving van were shut, safely guarding the remnants of the years gone by. We watched as the engines rumbled, the brakes released, and the van carried our worldly possessions off toward the highway aiming for Texas.

We said our goodbyes to our great neighbors and friends, the Fishbacks, and returned to the house for one last round of checks. With the closing and locking of every window, the past was being sealed. Closing and locking the door behind us, we descended the steps and landed on the sidewalk. Mixed emotions filled my heart, and tears tempted to fall. A lump welled up in my throat. The chapters of my childhood were soon coming to a close. Briefly standing on that sidewalk, my heart wanted to stay, but alas, the child had no choice.

"Jilene, hurry, we have a long drive ahead!"

"Okay, Dad!"

Shaken from my drifting thoughts, I quickly looked at Dad and jumped into my place in the back seat beside Kim and Terri. He flipped back the driver's seat of our two-door Impala, hopped in behind the wheel, and got the motor running. As Mom took her place, last-minute mental checks feebly floated from her lips, "Did I remember this, and did you do that?" Once the appraisal of the situation was settled, the car doors were hastily shut. Dad backed the car away from the redwood fence and pulled forward onto Delaware Avenue. He made that last U-turn north to turn west on Page Boulevard.

I quickly looked one last time at our house on the corner, 6300, to etch into my memory the two-story home with an attic and basement, the front yard where we had so many wonderful family times playing catch, having snowball fights, chasing friends, and celebrating with family and...in that short moment it all flooded back. As we rounded the corner, I saw my maple tree, and a smile came gently across my face. That was where Dad stood holding Kim, with Terri right beside him after Mom told him I was running away from home. I remembered his words as he waved goodbye, "Bye, Sissie! Have a nice time!" Now I was really leaving, but this time we were all leaving home! The late afternoon sun filtered a warm yellow glow as we headed west and south toward Texas. If the house and the tree could talk, would they have called out, "Bye, Jilene! Have a nice time!"

The End (for now)

Epilogue

*I*t is my hope that, in a glimpse of my childhood, you were encouraged to remember the beautiful things in your life. I chose to share these stories because they were the flowers in my garden of memories. As I wrote, many weeds popped up along the way, and each and every one had to be dealt with. What my parents told me about weeding is that if you do not destroy the roots, the weeds will come back. Some were very stubborn, and some took weeks to see, dig up, and destroy. Much soul-searching, prayer, acknowledgment of sin, repentance, and forgiveness were packed into the four years writing this book. Many tears of grief and happiness watered this garden, and God was faithful to hear my heart in each instance. You may wonder, "Why did you not include the weed stories?"

Each time I came across a weed or a patch of weeds, I had to stop and deal with them. I felt the need to listen to what the Holy Spirit kept bringing to my heart. It was a Bible verse that gave me the vision for writing.

Finally, brethren,
whatsoever things are true,
whatsoever things *are* honest,
whatsoever things *are* just,
whatsoever things *are* pure,

whatsoever things *are* lovely,
whatsoever things *are* of good report;
if *there be* any virtue,
and if *there be* any praise,
think on these things.

Philippians 4:8, KJV[B]

So as I worked the garden that became this book, my goal was to provide things that were honest, just, pure, lovely, and of good report. I looked back at the story about Pastor Biel when I told him, "Pastor, you are a good pastor!". He told me that he was not and that helped me realize I saw the flowers in his garden. I did not know the toil he went through and the weeds he removed. Nor was I there when God provided the water, the fertilizer, the storms, the droughts, the pestilence, and the sunshine. Yet I could see the flowers in his garden and was blessed in the experience. This was the virtue that came. And the praise? Oh yes, the praise goes to God who took us both through. In His Name is the glory for now and forevermore!

Notes

Chapter 2

1. The corner of Page Boulevard at Delaware Avenue is now listed as Page Avenue and Stephen Jones Avenue.

http://freepages.rootsweb.com/~haefner/history/streetnames/

Chapter 13

2. Grace Evangelical Lutheran Church was completed in 1910 at 6440 Easton Avenue on the west side of Wellston. Easton Avenue was changed to Martin Luther King Drive in 1972. The address number was changed to 6404 in 1972. The church is now Evangelist Center COGIC Grace Lutheran Church. Two other famous landmarks to the east of Grace were Central Hardware and Wellston State Bank. This information was found in a The Historic Buildings Survey Churches Built Before 1941 in Saint Louis County.

http://dnr.mo.gov/shpo/survey/SLAS026-R.pdf

Chapter 30

3. Read more: An old German poem we sang was "The Happy Wanderer" by Florenz Friedrich Sigismund (1788-1857). We sang it a little differently than the following original words. This site a list of many other scouting, patriotic, and campfire songs.

https://www.scoutsongs.com/lyrics/happywanderer.html

4. *Real Family Camping: 20 Favorite Campfire Songs for Kids.*

http://realfamilycamping.blogspot.com/2011/08/20-traditional-campfire-songs-for-kids.html

Chapter 40

5. Plan Your Visit - The Mark Twain Boyhood Home & Museum.

https://marktwainmuseum.org/plan-your-visit/

Chapter 43

6. "Lo, How a Rose E'er Blooming." Matthew 1:20-21; Hebrews 2:14-15; Luke 2:1-18, Source: German, 16th cent. (sts. 1-2, 4), Language: English, Tune Information, Name: ES IST EIN ROS (Rhythmic), Arranger: Michael Praetorius, 1571-1621, Meter: 76 76 6 76, Key: F Major, Source: Alte Catholische Geistliche Kirchengeseng, Köln, 1599.

https://hymnary.org/hymn/LSB2006/359

Chapter 48

7. Articles concerning The State Bank of Wellston

http://www.beltstl.com/tag/state-bank-of-wellston/

8. State Bank of Wellston History • Deconstruction

http://web.nationalbuildingarts.org/recovery-projects/banks/state-bank-of-wellston/

Chapter 59

9. This link is an interesting interview with an employee of The Glass House Restaurant named, Lavon Hightower Lewis. The Glass House Restaurant was built in 1957. It has gone through several changes, losing its once glamorous standing, complete with escalators and fine furnishings and fixtures, fancy restrooms with lipstick vending machines, to a quick stop for a McDonald's, Subway and Kum and Go Gas Stations. It is currently called the Will

Rogers Archway. It is slated for destruction as of 2020 with the redesign to enlarge the highway.

https://dc.library.okstate.edu/digital/collection/glasshouse/id/7/

Bible References

The Bible verses referred to in *A Heart Full of Precious Memories,* are from the The Holy Scriptures, King James Version. They are listed here with a link to www.blueletterbible.org. Ebook version readers may click on the underlined verse addresses to get access to the references.

<u>Quotations and About the Author</u>

A. Matthew 5:16 "Matthew 5, KJV- Let your light so shine." Cited 4 Sep 2020.

https://www.blueletterbible.org/kjv/mat/5/16/s_934016

<u>Quotations and Epilogue</u>

B. Philippians 4:8 "Philippians 4, KJV- Finally brethren whatsoever things are." Cited 4 Sep 2020.

https://www.blueletterbible.org/kjv/phl/4/8/s_1107008

<u>Chapter 22</u>

C. Revelation 3:20 "Revelation 3, KJV- Behold I stand at the." Cited 4 Sep 2020.

https://www.blueletterbible.org/kjv/rev/3/20/s_1170020

<u>Chapter 43</u>

D. John 3:16 "John 3, KJV- For God so loved the." Cited 4 Sep 2020.

https://www.blueletterbible.org/kjv/jhn/3/16/s_1000016

Chapter 44

E. Numbers 6:24-26 "Numbers 6, KJV- The LORD bless thee and." Cited 4 Sep 2020.

https://www.blueletterbible.org/kjv/num/6/24/s_123024

Chapter 59

F. Acts 17:11 "Acts 17, KJV- These were more noble than." Cited 4 Sep 2020.

https://www.blueletterbible.org/kjv/act/17/11/s_1035011

Acknowledgements

Some wonderful people fearlessly encouraged me during the process of writing and the production of *A Heart Full of Precious Memories*. I appreciate the time given, the love shared, the willingness to both support, and add truthful critique along the way. Their gifts are more precious memories worth sharing.

Steve Williams - Husband, best friend, and terrific sounding board! You were the first to hear every word. Your responses were unforgettable Your laughter and tears were genuine. You prodded me to write and enjoyed every minute of the process. You have been my number one encourager! I love you dearly!

Sheila Armstrong - The first to read the book, share the memories, and enlighten me on some shared childhood experiences. Your laughter and air hugs mean the world to me! I so appreciate all you did to encourage me! Thank you, "Sista Cousin!"

Virginia Ritterbusch - Accountability Partner. You helped me stay on track, celebrated victories, and bandaged my heartache and frustrations along the way! Thank you for your faithfulness for over four years!

Christine Garland - Memoir Coach. Your unexpected desire to reach out and edit my first download of the ebook was amazing. You are a precious servant who I did not know was coming to make a difference! Thank you so much!

Barbara Saylors - Friend. Out of the clear blue sky, you offered to proofread my pre-published manuscript. Your insights were so helpful. I miss the many times we shared at Bible study and meals together. Neither of us knew you would be at home with Jesus so soon. Thank you dear friend!

I also want to thank a special group of people from Self-Publishing School who taught and encouraged me along the way: Chandler Bolt, Sean Sumner, Lise Cartwright, Gary Williams, Jed Jurchenko, and hundreds more both leaders and students. You have all added education and encouragement along this journey. I am grateful!

I thank God for the way He brings such precious people into our lives at just the right time! May their practical and emotional investments be blessed!

About the Author

JILENE WILLIAMS

Jilene Williams lives in Orlando, Florida, with her precious husband, Steve. They have enjoyed over four decades of marriage. They have been blessed with four children, their spouses, and twenty grandchildren and counting.

She is a memoir writer who feels that God gave her three blessings to share: a heartwarming smile, the ability to encourage, and a goal to make her husband laugh everyday. Her motto is, "The world is a better place when you warm another's heart." Also one of her favorite Bible verses is, "Let your light so shine before men that they may see your good works and glorify your Father which is in heaven." Matthew 5:16, KJVᴬ˙

Jilene was born in St. Louis, Missouri, and spent most of her first twelve years there.

Bible study, writing, photography, crafts, sewing, singing, and teaching are among Jilene's activities. She especially enjoys them when others are involved.

For more information, Jilene may be reached by:

Email: jilene@jilene.com

Website: www.jilene.com

Newsletter and free download sign up:

www.jilene.com/heartwarmersmembers

Will You Help Me Spread the Word?

I want to personally thank you for taking this journey with me!

There are two things that you could do to help share

A Heart Full of Precious Memories

1 - Recommend it to your friends.

2 - Please give your honest review on

www.amazon.com

and

www.goodreads.com

Thank you so very much for your help!

Made in the USA
Columbia, SC
22 May 2021